INSTANT PAPER TOYS

To Pop, Spin, Whirl & Fly

• • •

INSTANT PAPER TOYS
To Pop, Spin, Whirl & Fly

•••••

E. Richard Churchill

Illustrated by Dennis Kendrick

Sterling Publishing Co., Inc.   New York

Edited by Robert Hernandez

Library of Congress Cataloging-in-Publication Data

Churchill, E. Richard (Elmer Richard)
  Instant paper toys.

  Includes index.
  Summary: Illustrated, step-by-step instructions for
making a variety of playthings out of paper and other
simple materials. Includes such objects as paper
airplanes, noisemakers, boomerangs, pinwheels, and
others.
    1. Paper work—Juvenile literature.   2. Handicraft—
Juvenile literature.   [1. Paper work.   2. Handicraft]
I. Kendrick, Dennis, ill.   II. Title.
TT870.C545   1986   745.54   85-26229
ISBN 0-8069-6276-3
ISBN 0-8069-6277-1 (lib. bdg.)

Contents

For Eric and Sean, who always take delight in helping.

And for the hundreds and even thousands of students who helped without realizing it.

What This Book Is All About

Do you enjoy creating things that pop, that fly, or that spin through the air?

Do you like making noise?

Do you think it's fun to turn a piece of paper or other simple things into terrific toys?

Do you like being the first person to come up with something that your friends haven't seen or done before?

If you answered "yes" to any or all of these questions, read on. This is your kind of book.

METRIC EQUIVALENCY CHART

MM—MILLIMETRES   CM—CENTIMETRES

INCHES TO MILLIMETRES AND CENTIMETRES

INCHES	MM	CM	INCHES	CM	INCHES	CM
⅛	3	0.3	9	22.9	30	76.2
¼	6	0.6	10	25.4	31	78.7
⅜	10	1.0	11	27.9	32	81.3
½	13	1.3	12	30.5	33	83.8
⅝	16	1.6	13	33.0	34	86.4
¾	19	1.9	14	35.6	35	88.9
⅞	22	2.2	15	38.1	36	91.4
1	25	2.5	16	40.6	37	94.0
1¼	32	3.2	17	43.2	38	96.5
1½	38	3.8	18	45.7	39	99.1
1¾	44	4.4	19	48.3	40	101.6
2	51	5.1	20	50.8	41	104.1
2½	64	6.4	21	53.3	42	106.7
3	76	7.6	22	55.9	43	109.2
3½	89	8.9	23	58.4	44	111.8
4	102	10.2	24	61.0	45	114.3
4½	114	11.4	25	63.5	46	116.8
5	127	12.7	26	66.0	47	119.4
6	152	15.2	27	68.6	48	121.9
7	178	17.8	28	71.1	49	124.5
8	203	20.3	29	73.7	50	127.0

YARDS TO METRES

YARDS	METRES	YARDS	METRES	YARDS	METRES	YARDS	METRES	YARDS	METRES
⅛	0.11	2⅛	1.94	4⅛	3.77	6⅛	5.60	8⅛	7.43
¼	0.23	2¼	2.06	4¼	3.89	6¼	5.72	8¼	7.54
⅜	0.34	2⅜	2.17	4⅜	4.00	6⅜	5.83	8⅜	7.66
½	0.46	2½	2.29	4½	4.11	6½	5.94	8½	7.77
⅝	0.57	2⅝	2.40	4⅝	4.23	6⅝	6.06	8⅝	7.89
¾	0.69	2¾	2.51	4¾	4.34	6¾	6.17	8¾	8.00
⅞	0.80	2⅞	2.63	4⅞	4.46	6⅞	6.29	8⅞	8.12
1	0.91	3	2.74	5	4.57	7	6.40	9	8.23
1⅛	1.03	3⅛	2.86	5⅛	4.69	7⅛	6.52	9⅛	8.34
1¼	1.14	3¼	2.97	5¼	4.80	7¼	6.63	9¼	8.46
1⅜	1.26	3⅜	3.09	5⅜	4.91	7⅜	6.74	9⅜	8.57
1½	1.37	3½	3.20	5½	5.03	7½	6.86	9½	8.69
1⅝	1.49	3⅝	3.31	5⅝	5.14	7⅝	6.97	9⅝	8.80
1¾	1.60	3¾	3.43	5¾	5.26	7¾	7.09	9¾	8.92
1⅞	1.71	3⅞	3.54	5⅞	5.37	7⅞	7.20	9⅞	9.03
2	1.83	4	3.66	6	5.49	8	7.32	10	9.14

•1•
Flying Gizmos and
Paper Planes

Whirly-Twirly

To make a whirly-twirly, start with a square of paper about 5 inches on each side. Fold it diagonally to form two triangles. Cut along this fold to separate the triangles (Illus. 1).

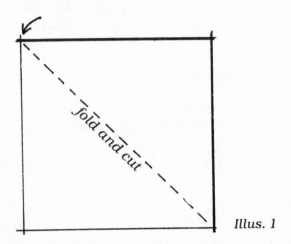

Illus. 1

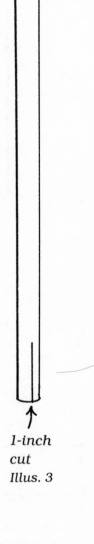

1-inch
cut
Illus. 3

Next fold point A underneath so it touches point C. Crease the fold. Point A is now under point C (Illus. 2).

Fold point B upwards to point C. This leaves point B on the top of the rest of the paper.

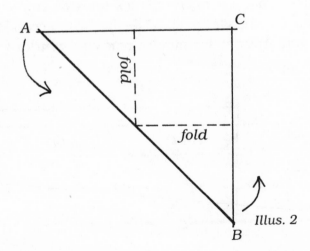

Illus. 2

With a pair of scissors, cut a slit in one end of a plastic straw (Illus. 3). Make the slit about 1 inch long. Cut both sides of the straw at the same time. This saves work and

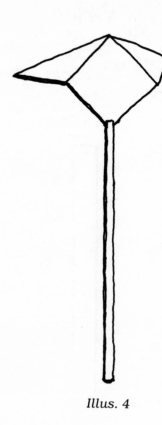

also helps make certain the slit is the same length on both sides of the straw.

Slip point C of the whirly-twirly into the slit you just cut in the straw. Allow points A and B to remain free. They are the whirly-twirly's wings.

Give the whirly-twirly a little toss into the air. Don't throw it so hard that the paper slips out of the straw. It will come down spinning rapidly (Illus. 4).

Paper Helicopter

It is easy to make a paper helicopter. First cut a strip of paper about 1½ inches wide. Make it as long as a sheet of notebook paper.

Next make the three cuts along the solid lines as shown in Illus. 5.

Fold end A up ⅛ inch and crease it well. Then fold the bottom over the first fold and crease it again. Do this twice. This helps make the end stiff and adds a little weight to the bottom.

Now fold the bottom part of the whirler along the dotted line in Illus. 5 from end A up to cut 1. Fold the other side from end A to cut 2 in the same way. The edges of the two folds will overlap each other.

Hold the helicopter by end A with cut 3 pointing straight upwards. Fold one of the blades towards you along the dotted line as shown in Illus. 5. Fold the second blade away from you. Your helicopter is ready to whirl.

Illus. 4

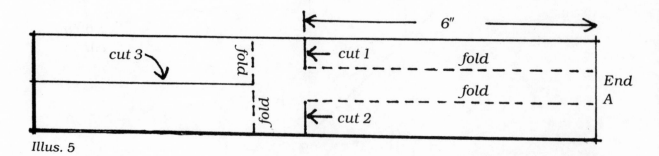

Illus. 5

Raise the helicopter above your head and then drop it. Watch it spin towards the ground. After flying it a few times, do some experiments. Cut several more. Make one with longer blades than your first model. Make another with shorter blades. When you fly these new ones you will find that the length of the blades makes a difference in the number of turns it will make.

Now slip a paper clip onto the bottom of a helicopter (Illus. 6). This added weight makes a difference in the speed of its descent. Paper helicopters are great fun on the playground, especially if a little breeze is blowing.

Illus. 6

Twirlicopter

This simple twirlicopter takes about two minutes to make and is a lot of fun to play with.

From a piece of stiff cardboard, such as a manila folder, cut out a propeller blade which looks similar to the one in Illus. 7. Don't worry about making it exact, but try to come close.

Illus. 7. Actual size.

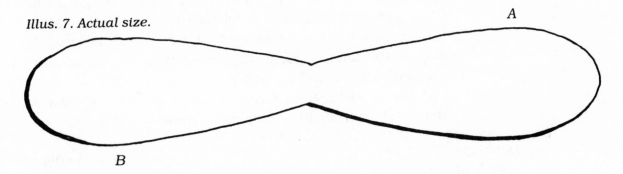

A

B

Here is a helpful hint. Since both ends of the blade should be alike, first make a pattern out of notebook paper. Double the paper and draw half the blade. Cut it out with the paper still folded (Illus. 8).

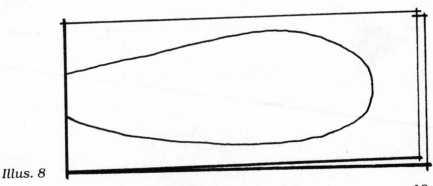

Illus. 8

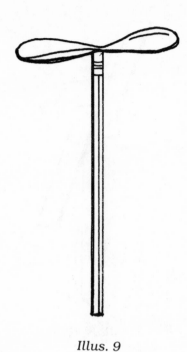

Illus. 9

After you cut out the blade and unfold it to its full length, carefully begin raising sides A and B. This gives the blade "lift" when it spins.

Start with side A. Carefully roll the edge of the blade around a pencil so it is slightly higher than the opposite side. Don't crease the blade. Just try to roll it up part way. Do the same for side B. Try to get sides A and B to rise the same distance in this manner.

To finish your twirlicopter, you need a long pencil with an eraser. It must be fairly long so you can easily hold it between your hands. Press a thumbtack through the center of the blade and stick it as far as possible into the eraser (Illus. 9). A Tinkertoy stick works well instead of a pencil unless the little slot at the end is too wide to hold the tack.

Your twirlicopter is ready to test. Place the pencil between the palms of your hands with the blade pointing upwards. Rapidly slide one hand past the other. The pencil between your hands will spin rapidly. As you let go of the pencil, give it a little toss. If all goes well, it should gain a little altitude and then whirl and twirl its way towards earth. If the tack is not in tightly enough, the blade won't turn. Press it in and try again.

Try blades of different sizes and see how well each works. Just don't use all the new pencils making twirlicopters.

Don't use your best pencil when you make this.

That's silly. To make the best twirlicopter, use your best pencil.

14

World's Easiest Glider

This simple glider is a breeze to make. Begin with a 4 ×
6 file card. If you don't have a file card handy, use stiff paper. Notebook paper will work fine, but don't use an entire
sheet—use a 4 × 6-inch piece.

Fold the card or piece of paper lengthwise down the middle. Then draw the glider design as shown in Illus. 10.
Don't worry about copying the design exactly, but draw it
as similar as possible.

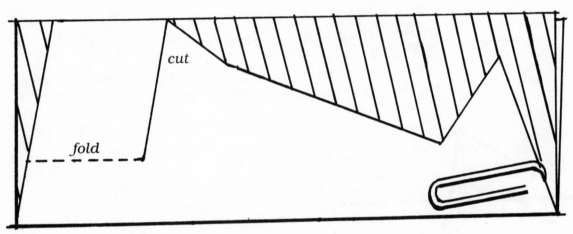

Illus. 10. Actual size.

After you draw the design, keep the card or paper folded
while you cut away the shaded area with a pair of scissors
(the paper clip is attached later). Now cut down about two-
thirds (or even three-fourths) of the way as indicated in the
drawing. Make this cut while the card or paper is still
folded so the two wings will be of equal size. Fold each
wing downwards and crease it.

Now slip a paper clip over the nose of the glider so it
holds both sides together. With the paper clip firmly in
place, make sure the wings stand out horizontally from the
body of the glider. Give it a quick toss and watch it make
its first flight.

If you used notebook paper for the glider, you will hear a
buzzing sound if you toss the glider hard enough, which
comes from the vibration of the wings. A glider made from
a card or from stiff paper won't buzz, but it will probably
fly farther.

The following are some ways to change later models of the world's easiest glider. Make a model with narrower wings. Make one in which the wing cut is not quite so deep, which results in shorter wings. Make the body a little smaller. Try a glider with two paper clips on its nose.

Happy glider flying!

Quick-Fold Glider

Begin with a sheet of notebook paper. Fold it lengthwise down the middle, then unfold it.

Now fold the two upper corners towards the center and crease them into place. Your glider should look like the one in Illus. 11.

Next fold point A towards the middle and crease it firmly. Do the same for point B (Illus. 12).

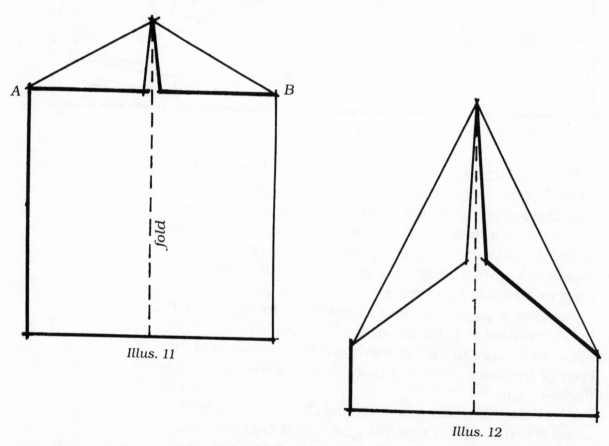

Illus. 11

Illus. 12

Refold your glider along the middle crease and place it on its side as shown in Illus. 13.

Fold the top side (along the dotted line in Illus. 13) so it reaches the bottom. Crease it firmly. Turn the glider over and do the same with the other side. Now that you have constructed the glider's wings, it's ready to fly.

Hold it as shown in Illus. 14 and give it a quick toss. It will fly for quite a distance.

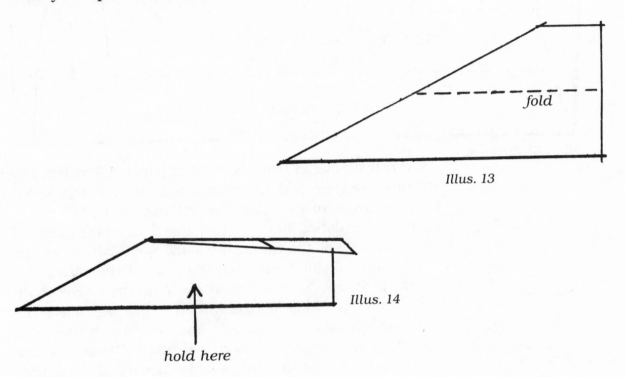

Illus. 13

Illus. 14

hold here

After you've made a few quick-fold gliders, try one with narrower paper. See how this changes the way the glider flies.

Change the sizes of the folds. For example, in Illus. 11 do not fold points A and B all the way to the middle. How does this change the way your glider behaves?

For another experiment, after you fold the wings downwards in Illus. 13, fold ½ inch of the outside edges of both wings upwards. This creates a different glider.

Darter

Fold a 4 × 6 file card lengthwise. If you don't have a file card, use stiff paper of the same size. (Regular notebook paper just doesn't seem to work very well.)

17

Draw your darter so it looks like the one in Illus. 15. Don't worry about being exact—it's just a general idea.

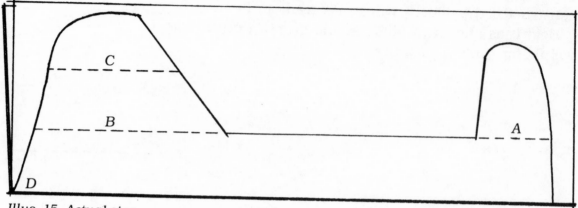

Illus. 15. Actual size.

Cut out the darter with the card or paper still folded. You are now ready to fold the wings and tail. Put the folded darter in front of you. Fold the top side of the tail downwards along dotted line A. Turn the darter over and fold the other side of the tail in the same way. This leaves the tail sections sticking out from the body of the darter.

Next pick up the darter and open the body. Fold both wings *inward* along dotted line B. This will make the wings touch inside the glider. Now fold the top halves of the wings downwards along dotted line C. What you now have is a darter with its wings folded inward at the bottom and outward at the top. But they should not stick straight out like the tail sections.

Place two paper clips at point D on the darter's nose as shown in Illus. 16. Put one clip on either side. *Do not* clip

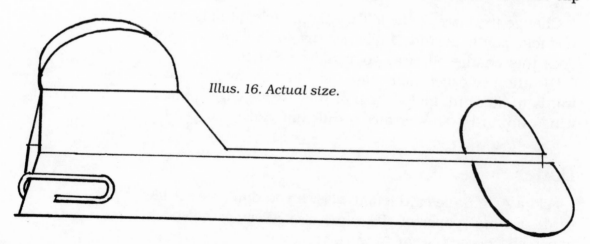

Illus. 16. Actual size.

the two sides together. The body of the darter should re-main open, although you may squeeze it together a bit when you launch it.

Give the darter a quick toss and off it goes. Experiment by bending the tail flaps a bit more upwards or down-wards. Adjust the wings by bending them more inward or the tips outward. Raise one a bit and lower the other. Do the same for the tail flaps.

You may want to make other darters with larger or smaller tails. Make similar changes in the wings. Experi-ment until you find the perfect combination.

Paper Plane

A sheet of notebook paper makes an excellent paper glider. Just do a little folding and your glider is ready to fly.

Fold the paper lengthwise down the middle. Crease it, then flatten the paper out (Illus. 17). Use the middle fold for a guide line. Now fold the two upper corners towards the middle and crease them as shown in Illus. 18.

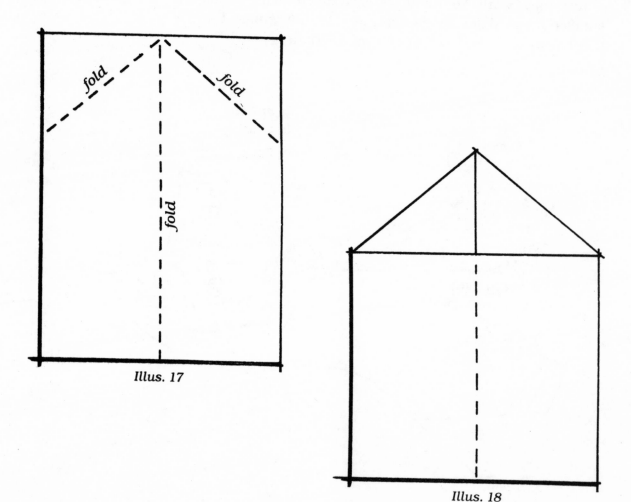

Illus. 17

Illus. 18

For the next step, fold the triangular part of the paper towards you as shown in Illus. 19.

Next fold the top right corner towards the center line and crease it. Do the same with the top left corner. Your glider should look like the one in Illus. 20.

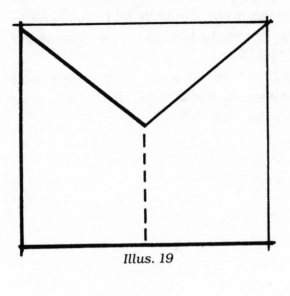

Illus. 19

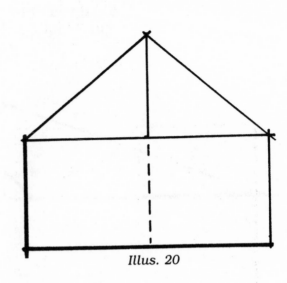

Illus. 20

Don't give up now. Your glider is all but completed. Make the two folds at the dotted lines as shown in Illus. 21. After you do these folds your glider should look like Illus. 22.

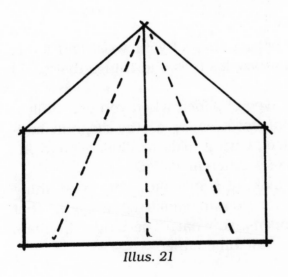

Illus. 21

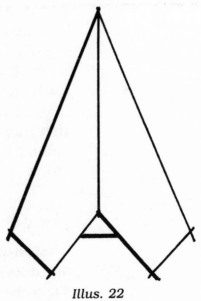

Illus. 22

Fold the glider along the original middle fold, this time in the opposite direction. It should look like Illus. 23, which shows a side view of the glider.

Take hold of the center fold between your thumb and forefinger. Pull the wings upwards into place and your glider should look like the one in Illus. 24.

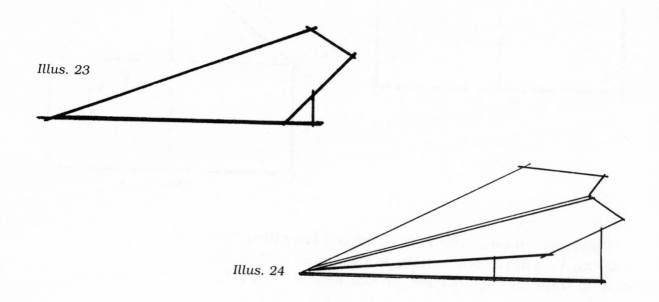

Illus. 23

Illus. 24

Launch your glider with a snap of your wrist and it will sail away. Watch out for people's eyes and things that could break when you fly it.

To make a different type of glider, when you get to Illus. 19, don't fold the point down as far as the diagram indicates. Try slightly different wing folds in Illus. 20 and 21. Each change will make a different glider.

Don't be afraid of making a mistake. The worst thing that can happen is for you to construct a glider that doesn't fly. If that happens, so what? The Wright brothers didn't get it right the first time either.

Looper

Most paper airplanes or gliders fly a far distance. This one does not. It always flies in one loop and comes back to the same place.

Start with an 8½-inch square of notebook paper. Fold it in half diagonally as shown in Illus. 25. Crease the paper and unfold it. Then make the two side folds as indicated. Crease these folds and do not unfold the glider. It should look like Illus. 26.

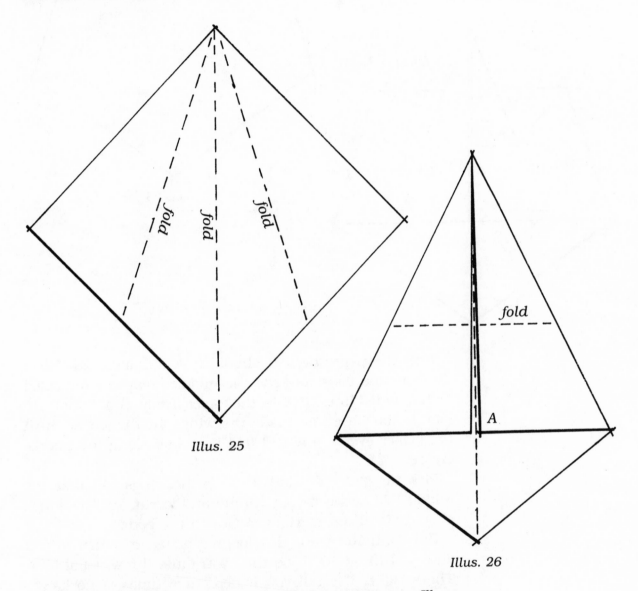

Illus. 25

Illus. 26

Fold the tail down as shown by the dotted line in Illus. 26. Make sure the point of the tail extends about 1½ inches past point A as shown in the illustration.

Next fold the tail upwards so the tip of it extends about an inch above the body of the glider. This is indicated in Illus. 27. Now fold the tip of the tail downwards about ½ inch as shown by the dotted line in Illus. 27.

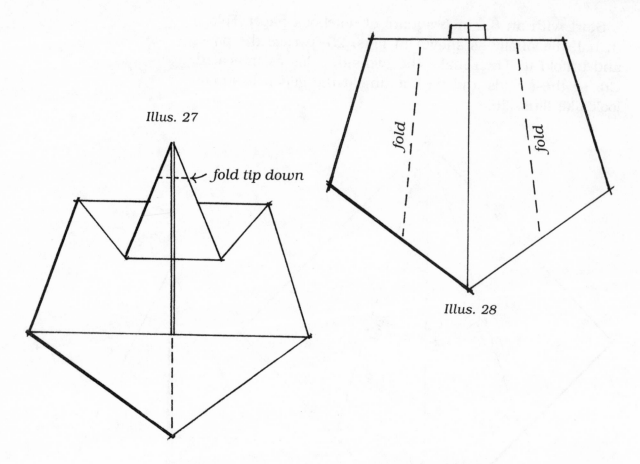

Illus. 27

fold tip down

fold

fold

Illus. 28

Turn the paper over. It should look like Illus. 28. Make the two side folds towards the middle crease as indicated by the dotted lines. Crease the paper firmly, and do not unfold it. You have just made the wings for the looper. Turn the looper over again and fold it in half along the middle crease.

Pick the glider up and turn up the wings. Squeeze the middle fold between your thumb and forefinger. The wings should stand out at right angles to the body.

But wait! You want this looping glider to return to you after you throw it. To do this, you must throw it tail first. That's right. The tail you folded three times is no longer the tail. It is now the nose of the glider as shown in Illus. 29.

Throw your finished glider *straight upward*. It will make one loop and come right back to you. Do not throw it forward like a regular paper airplane. If you do, it will fly towards the ground. (Go ahead! Try flying it like a regular glider just to see what happens!)

You may want to try some changes when you build your next looping glider. Change the wings by making the wing fold not exactly in the middle. Make the tail (actually the nose) a bit longer. See how these changes affect the way the glider loops.

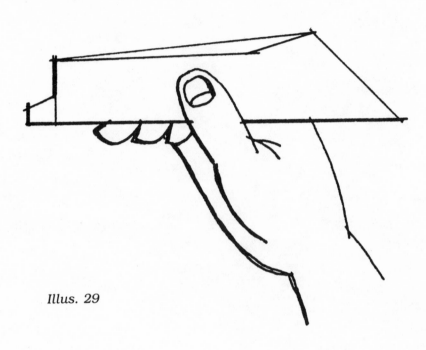

Illus. 29

Paper planes are fun. Just don't make too many of them.

•2•
Instant Action

Screamer

It takes about one minute to make a screamer. In five more seconds you can learn how to use it. Then you can make fantastic sounds with it for hours.

Cut a piece of paper about 1½ × 3¼ inches. Fold A and B towards you about ½ inch from each end, as shown in Illus. 30. Fold C in the opposite direction in the middle.

Next, cut a slit in the middle of fold C about ½ inch long as shown. Your screamer is now ready to use. It should stand on the table like the one in Illus. 31.

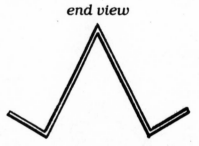

end view

Illus. 31. Actual size.

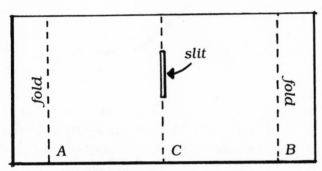

Illus. 30. Actual size.

Hold the screamer between your index and middle fingers. Put the bottom flaps against your lips with the slit pointing away from you. Now blow into the screamer (Illus. 32).

The vibration of the paper will cause the screamer to make a most unusual sound. Blow harder or softer—tighten your fingers—loosen them a bit and vary the sound.

Experiment with some paper that is stiff and with some that is fairly thin. Make the slit and folds slightly larger or a little smaller.

This is one of the easiest of all noisemakers to construct and one of the most fun to use.

Illus. 32

Cellophane Whistle

A little piece of cellophane cut from a candy wrapper or from any food package can be turned into a fantastic whistle. It makes a shrill sound which is great fun.

Hold a 2-inch square or rectangle of cellophane between

the thumb and forefinger of each hand. Grasp it firmly right at the edges (Illus. 33). Stretch it tight but don't pull hard enough to tear it. If your whistle rips or tears, cut another piece and try it again.

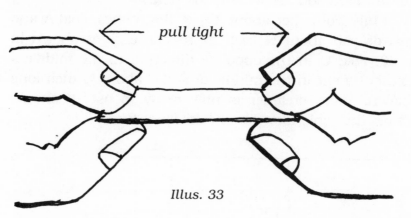

← *pull tight* →

Illus. 33

Be careful where you use this noisemaker. Some people won't like it.

Rest the sides of your thumbs and forefingers on either side of your mouth. Tighten your lips into a straight line. Open the center of your lips just enough to form a little air passage and place the stretched edge of the cellophane directly in front it. Hold the cellophane between your lips but don't let it touch either one.

Now blow a stream of air directly at the edge of the cellophane. The result will surprise you. The force of the air causes the cellophane to vibrate, making a shrill whistle. Keep your lips tight and the stream of air narrow. Adjust the position of the cellophane upwards or downwards, closer to your lips or further away, until you get the best sound. Tighten or loosen your hold on the cellophane to vary the tone. Anyone can do this, so don't give up if your cellophane does not whistle at first.

Try using several different kinds of paper. Cellophane vibrates fastest and makes the highest tone. Magazine paper or notebook paper also works as a whistle, but it makes a completely different noise.

Singing Glass

A drinking glass can become an amazing noisemaker. All you have to do is to have the right glass and know how to use it.

Moisten the rim of a drinking glass. Make sure there are no chips in the rim. After it is wet all the way around, hold the glass in one hand. Begin to rub the pad of your finger back and forth along one section of the rim (Illus. 34). Within a few seconds, the glass should begin to squeak and sing. The more you rub the louder and higher pitched the sound becomes.

Some glasses work better than others. Some do not sing or squeak at all. It is just a matter of trial and error until you find one which works. Generally, the thinner the sides of the glass the better the sound. Experiment with a few different glasses. But don't use any expensive crystal without asking permission from an adult.

Once the glass begins to squeak, try rubbing faster or slower. Vary the pressure of your finger. Make the rim wetter or try it a bit drier. Pretty soon you will find the combination that makes the best sound.

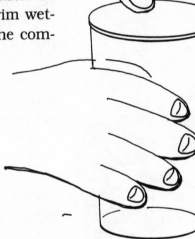

Hoot, Toot, and Whistle

Illus. 34

Empty bottles make excellent noisemakers. All you need is a 2-liter soft-drink bottle to have your own steamboat whistle. The plastic container works just fine.

Place your mouth on the lip of the bottle as shown in Illus. 35. Inhale deeply and blow *downwards* into the bottle. Keep both lips tight and blow strongly and steadily. If you do not hear a deep hoot after you blow, adjust your upper lip and try again. The art of bottle tooting is to blow directly downwards into the bottle.

31

Not everyone wants to make a toot like a steamboat. If this is the case, use a smaller bottle. The smaller the bottle the higher the hoot or whistle you create.

As an experiment, listen to the sound made by whichever container you are using for your hooting. Then run some water into it. Blow again. The tone will be higher than before.

Illus. 35

Cool Fans

A paper fan is easy to make and can be useful as well. What is more, if an entire classroom of students sit and fan themselves after gym class or lunch break, a teacher may go out of his or her mind.

Start with a sheet of notebook paper. Place it flat on the desk in front of you with the narrower side of the paper nearest you. Fold the edge about ½ inch and crease the paper. Turn the sheet over and fold another ½ inch in the same manner. Repeat this until the entire paper forms a little accordion ½ inch wide and as long as the paper. (This is called an accordion fold, by the way. You can see why.)

Grasp one end of the folded paper firmly between your thumb and forefinger. Fan out the top part. Gently move your paper fan back and forth and feel the cooling breeze.

Keep an eye on your teacher and put your fan away if you get an angry look.

Do you want to be cool or not? I vote for cool before careful.

Belt Snapper

Do you have a belt which is not doing anything more useful than holding your pants up? Put it to use doing something more fun. Just slip it out of its loops and turn it into a belt snapper.

Double the belt so you can hold the two loose ends in one hand and the folded end in the other. Move your hands together so the two halves of the belt separate in the middle (Illus. 36). Make sure one rises and the other half drops when you do this.

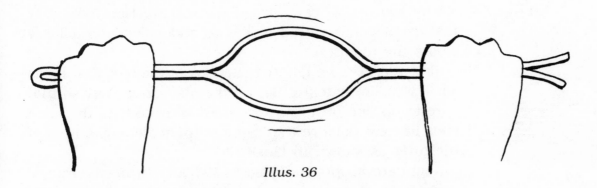

Illus. 36

Now jerk your hands apart quickly and firmly. Remember to hold onto the ends of the belt. You will hear a loud snap or pop. Try again, jerking it harder and faster. Soon you will learn to create a really loud pop.

Try snapping belts of different widths. It will also work with strips of certain kinds of plastic banding material. Be careful not to use anything which can cut your hands when it slides and slips in your fist.

Straw-Cover Rocket

Individual plastic drinking straws usually are covered with jackets of very thin paper. To make a little rocket, carefully open one end of the paper covering and tear off about ½ inch of paper. Do not open the other end. Leave the jacket on the straw, fill your lungs with air, and put your lips on the opened end. Now take aim and blow. The straw's cover will become a tiny rocket that shoots towards the target of your choice.

Even if the little paper jackets are not available, you can still make your own straw rocket. Simply cut a piece of paper about 8 inches long and 1½ inches wide. Use paper as thin as you can find. Tissue paper is excellent. The lighter the rocket the more distance you can propel it. Roll it around a pencil or a plastic straw. Use tape to keep it from unrolling and to seal one end.

Slip your rocket over a straw, aim, and blow. This handmade cover may be used over and over.

Fabulous Flying Matchbox

Very few people can turn down a dare. Here is a dare that usually ends with a matchbox suddenly flying halfway across the room.

First you need an empty matchbox of the type that holds small wooden matches. Set up the matchbox cover so that it rests on one of its narrow sides with both of the open ends in view. Balance the inside of the matchbox on top of the cover as shown in Illus. 37.

Now dare anyone to make a fist and bring it straight down hard on the balanced matchbox. Tell the person that you don't think he or she is strong enough to smash the matchbox in one blow.

Tell everyone that unless the blow is struck good and hard, the matchbox will just fly away instead of being smashed.

Who can turn down a dare like this? The wonderful thing is that when the box is hit the two parts become the famous, fabulous, flying matchbox.

Try this yourself, then look for friends to accept your dare. You can use the same matchbox again and again.

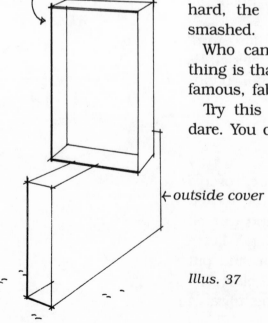

inside box

outside cover

Illus. 37

•3•
Snappers, Cracklers, and Poppers

Little Paper Snapper

To construct a little paper snapper, you need a square of stiff paper. A heavy-duty grocery bag (one of the big ones) from the supermarket works just fine. Cut a piece of paper about 8 or 9 inches square. Fold the paper in half and crease it firmly.

Open the paper out flat as shown in Illus. 38. Take the right-hand edge and fold it towards the middle crease. Fold and crease it so it looks like Illus. 39.

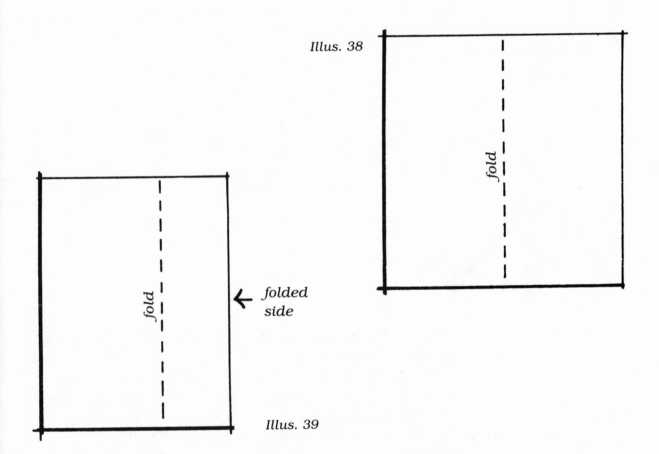

Illus. 38

fold

← *folded side*

fold

Illus. 39

Once more open the paper flat. Now fold the right-hand edge towards the new fold you just made. Crease it. (The fold should be about an inch wide.) Do not unfold it this time. Instead fold it over again. This is easy because you fold along the crease made in Illus. 39. Fold it over one more time and crease it. You should now have a rectangle looking like Illus. 40. The left-hand side of the paper is still flat. The right-hand side is four layers thick.

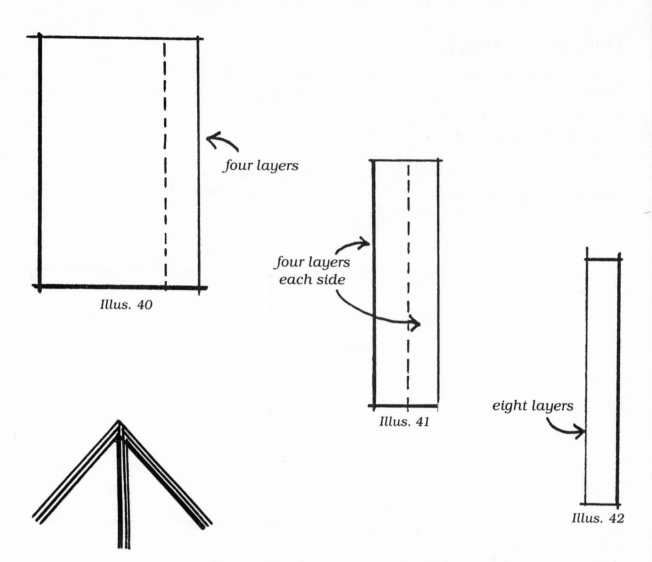

four layers

Illus. 40

*four layers
each side*

Illus. 41

eight layers

Illus. 42

Illus. 43

Do exactly the same for the left-hand side as you did for the right. This gives you four layers of paper on each side of the middle fold in Illus. 41. Now fold both sides together along the middle fold as shown in Illus. 42. You should have a long, narrow piece of paper eight layers thick.

Now cut halfway down the original middle fold with a pair of scissors. Then fold the right-hand four layers down as far as the cut and crease the paper sharply. Do the same for the other side, creasing it in the opposite direction. This gives you a pair of drooping rabbit's ears as shown in Illus. 43.

Your little paper snapper is ready for use. Take a firm hold on the bottom of the snapper with your thumb and index finger. Hold the other hand higher on the base and just below the point where the two loose flaps join. Jerk down sharply with your thumb and index finger (see Illus. 44). This pulls the snapper between your fingers. The two flaps snap together. Your snapper snaps and you are in business.

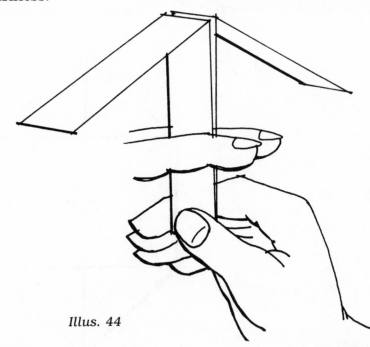

Illus. 44

After a snap or two, you will probably have to fold the two flaps down again. The sharper you jerk down on the snapper the louder it snaps. Practice it a few times and you will see how best to hold your fingers and how hard to pull.

Do this long enough and someone is certain to tell you to stop.

Live it up. Put some snap into your life.

Paper Popper

You can make the big paper popper out of a sheet of notebook paper. But since you want this to be a BIG popper, use a sheet of newspaper.

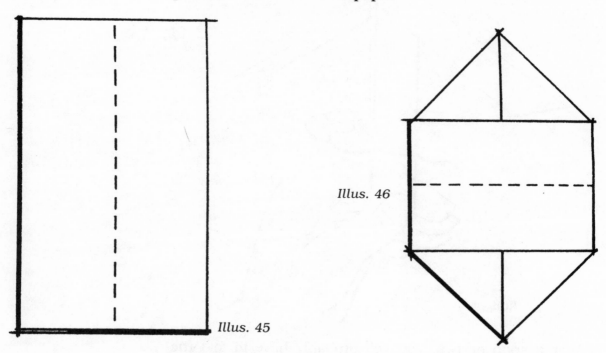

Illus. 46

Illus. 45

Fold it lengthwise down the middle so the narrow end is towards you. Make a good crease and unfold the paper (Illus. 45). Then fold each of the corners towards the middle and crease them into place (Illus. 46).

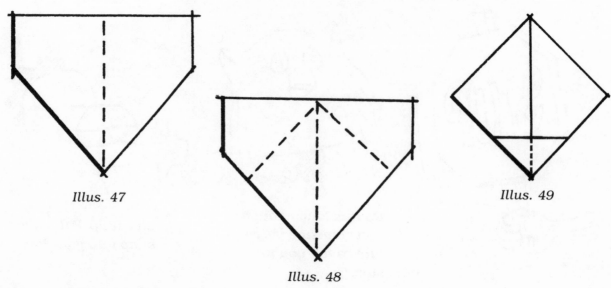

Illus. 47

Illus. 49

Illus. 48

Fold the top point down to the bottom point. Crease it so it stays in place (Illus. 47). Now fold the right-hand corner down so it aligns with the middle crease. Make this fold good and sharp. Do the same for the left-hand corner (Illus. 48).

Your popper should look like Illus. 49.

Unfold the two flaps you just folded in Illus. 49. Turn the popper over. Now fold the two corners down and crease them just like you did in Illus. 48. Your popper should

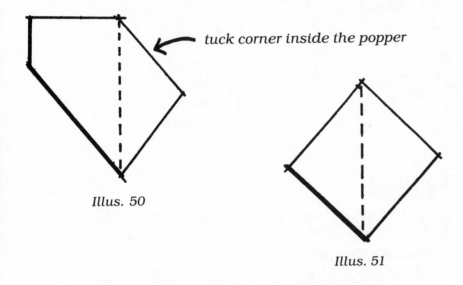

tuck corner inside the popper

Illus. 50

Illus. 51

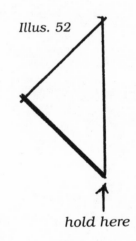

Illus. 52

hold here

again look like Illus. 49. Unfold the two flaps just as you did before. Your popper again looks like it did in Illus. 48.

Hold the popper by the bottom points. Tuck the upper right-hand corner inward so that the corner is now *inside* the popper (Illus. 50).

Tuck in the upper left-hand corner in the same way and your popper looks like Illus. 51. Fold the right-hand side along the old middle crease so it looks like a triangle (Illus. 52).

Your big paper popper is ready to pop. Hold the bottom point between your thumb and forefinger. Don't let go. Snap your hand and wrist downwards sharply. The tucked-in parts of the popper will snap out. The popper should make a loud pop. If the popper is large enough, it will make an extremely loud pop. To use it again, tuck in the corners and snap it downwards.

Use the popper until it tears or "blows out." Then make a new one. Try shelving paper if you can get it. Experiment with various kinds of paper and different sizes.

Don't wear out your welcome with these poppers.

If people don't like it, they can cover their ears!

Big Bang

Begin with a square piece of paper—8 × 8 inches is a good size for your first big-bang paper popper.

First fold the paper diagonally and crease it. Unfold it and then fold the opposite diagonal. Unfold it and flatten out the paper so it looks like Illus. 53.

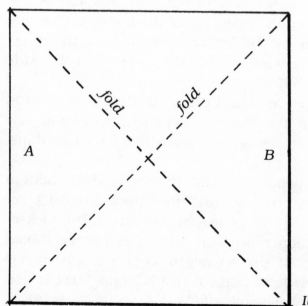

Illus. 53

Fold edge A towards edge B, making sure that the sides fold *inward*. Flatten the paper as you do so until A and B form the base of a triangle, as shown in Illus. 54.

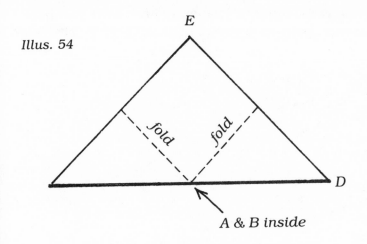

Illus. 54

E

D

A & B inside

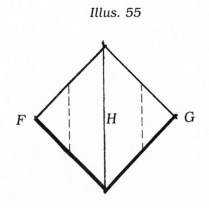

Illus. 55

F H G

Now fold the top layer of point C to point E and crease it into place. Fold the top layer of point D to point E in the same way. Then turn the popper over and repeat these steps for the other side. The popper should now look like a square, as shown in Illus. 55.

Fold the top layer of point F to the middle of line H and crease it. Fold the top layer of point G to H and crease it. Turn the popper over and repeat these steps for the other side. Your popper is almost ready to pop and should look like Illus. 56.

One of the pointed ends has a tiny opening in it. Find that end. It is either at K or L, as shown in Illus. 56.

Blow gently into that little opening. The folded paper popper will begin to form a paper box. Help it along by shaping it with the tips of your fingers. Once the box is formed, put a little piece of transparent or masking tape over the hole. Your popper is ready for the big event.

There should be little triangular "tails" at each end of the box. If you want to make the popper fancy, fold each small tail over and tuck it into the larger tail beside it.

Place the big-bang paper popper on a flat surface such as the top of a table or a desk. Hold your hand directly over it

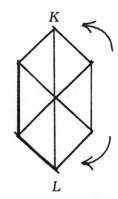

Illus. 56

K

L

blow in K or L

with your palm flat. Bring your hand down hard and strike the paper popper squarely (Illus. 57). You will hear a loud bang, which will cause heads to turn and maybe cause you to stay after school.

Now make a new big-bang paper popper and see how loudly you can make it explode.

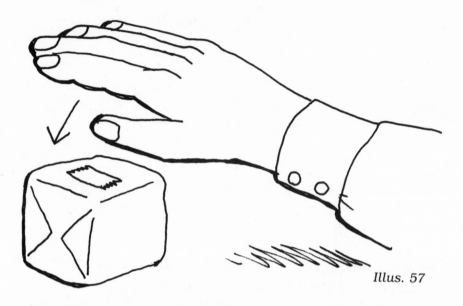

Illus. 57

Flying Palm Poppers

Cut or tear a square of paper about 1½ inches in size. Squeeze it into a wad and roll the wad between the palms of your hands. Straighten the paper out and then wad it up again a few more times until the little square of paper is rather limp. You have just made a palm popper (Illus. 58).

Illus. 58

Close one hand into a very loose fist. Leave enough room in the open part of your fist so that your bottom three fingers do *not* quite touch your palm. Your thumb should overlap your index finger so that the opening between them is about the size of a dime.

With the index finger of your other hand, push the square of paper up into the opening formed by your thumb and forefinger. Press the edges of the palm popper tightly against the lower edges of your thumb and finger. The palm popper should be shaped like a little dome, as shown in Illus. 59.

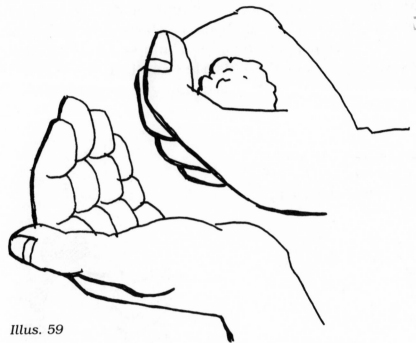

Illus. 59

Cup your free hand and bring it upwards in a rapid motion so that it strikes the open part of your hand with the palm popper in place (Illus. 59). If all goes well, you should hear a fairly loud popping sound. The little square of paper should fly into the air as the force of the compressed air sends it popping out of your hand.

If you do not get a pop and the palm popper stays in place, just try again. Adjust both hands to make an air-tight seal when they come together. Soon you will be able to make your palm popper work every time.

To make a fancier palm popper, tear or cut a piece of notebook paper about 1½ × 3½ inches. Wrap it around your index finger so that about half an inch sticks up past the end of your finger, as shown in Illus. 60.

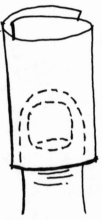

Illus. 60

Now use your other index finger and thumb to twist the open end of the paper into a tight twist on the top of your fingertip. This twist keeps the paper from unrolling and makes an air-tight pocket (Illus. 61).

Close one hand into a loose fist as you did for the first palm popper. Slip this new popper into place so that the twisted end sticks up from the space between your thumb and forefinger.

Illus. 61

45

Cup your other hand and bring your hands together just as you did before. The pop should be about the same. This new and better popper should sail into space. Some students who have worked at this can send their twisted palm poppers halfway across a classroom.

Some teachers may object when the air is full of palm poppers.

You may have a point. It's on top of your head.

Exploding Paper Bag

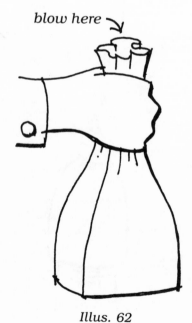

blow here ↘

Illus. 62

It is easy to make a paper-bag popper. Any paper bag that is not too large will work. Start with a bag about 9 or 10 inches tall. Gather the open end into one fist so that you can blow into it, as shown in Illus. 62.

Blow hard into the paper bag until it won't hold any more air. Quickly close your fist to trap the air inside. Give the bag a quarter twist if you wish.

With the open palm of your other hand, strike the bottom of the inflated bag so that your palm drives towards the bottom of your fist, holding the bag.

An explosive bang will occur and you will need to find another paper bag to pop.

You can make another good popper from a paper juice container. This kind of container is a miniature of the larger paper soft-drink containers.

Put the juice container on the floor with the open top down. Stamp your foot down hard on it, hitting it squarely. It will explode quite loudly.

Bursting Plastic Straw

You have just finished eating lunch at your favorite fast-food restaurant. Your plastic straw is in front of you. There is something to do with that straw which will make you the center of attention.

Take a firm grip on each end of the straw as shown in Illus. 63. Grasp both ends of the straw tightly between your thumbs and forefingers.

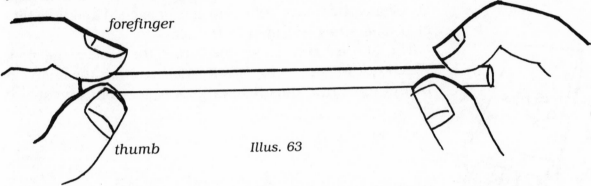

forefinger

thumb   *Illus. 63*

With one hand directly above the other, holding the ends of the straw tightly, wind your hands around and around. Each time you make one complete turn, the straw winds tightly around itself at each end. The distance between your hands becomes less and less as the straw winds up and becomes shorter. If you don't do this carefully, keeping your hands directly above each other, the straw won't wind up properly (Illus. 64).

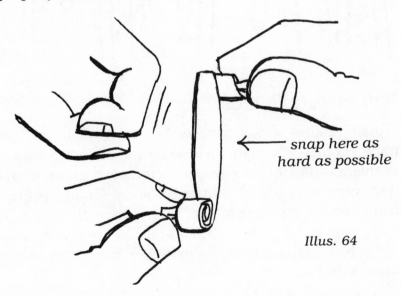

← *snap here as hard as possible*

Illus. 64

As you keep rotating your hands and winding up the straw, the air which is trapped inside it gets squeezed into a smaller and smaller space. When your straw has been wound up at both ends until only about 1½ inches remain, it is time to ask someone to burst it for you. Tell your friend to snap the straw with his index finger as hard as possible right in the middle (Illus. 64).

If you have done this properly and the finger snaps hard right in the middle of the straw, there will be a loud pop. People nearby will turn to see what happened and little bits of plastic straw will fly into the air.

The shorter you make the straw the louder the pop. Watch out for the flying plastic. Make certain the one who bursts the straw aims it towards a wall or out into space.

Rattlesnake Rattles

Just talking about rattlesnakes is enough to frighten most people. When you tell someone you have some rattlesnake rattles in an envelope, they want to see what you have even if it is just a little bit scary. Build up the suspense and warn people that the rattles are noisy. Then open your envelope of rattles and shake them out. The rattles whirr and jump and probably scare everyone out of their wits.

The rattles are easy to make. All you need are some small rubber bands, some metal washers, and hairpins or other stiff wire. Big paper clips will work nicely.

Bend the hairpins or clips to form a U-shape. Thread two rubber bands through the hole in the middle of a washer. Loop both ends of each band over one of the ends of the wire, as shown in Illus. 65. Now twist the washer around and around, until the rubber bands get tight. Make as many rattlers as you wish.

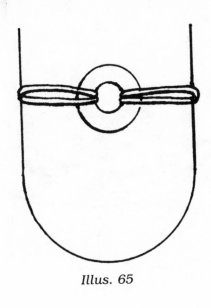

Illus. 65

Illus. 66

If you can't find a washer, don't give up. A key will work unless it is too long. Even a paper clip can be made to take the place of a washer, but it has to be kept lengthwse (Illus. 66).

Slip the wound-up rattlesnake rattles into an envelope so they don't unwind until you spill the rattles out onto a table or desk. If the washers start to unwind, hold the envelope flat so they don't spoil your trick.

You can also put these little rattles on a table under a book. When the book is lifted, the spinners go off with all sorts of jumping and thumping.

Practice emptying your rattles out of an envelope until

you are good at it. If you place them beneath books or other objects, make sure they are not on something which may be damaged, such as your family's new coffee table.

I suggest you not show this to any-one who is hold-ing something breakable.

W-why not?

·4·
Great Noisemakers

Turkey Caller

The only reason for naming this wonderful little device a turkey caller is because no one can think of a better name for it.

Begin with a piece of paper about 3¼ × 4 inches. Cut out the two shaded areas, as shown in Illus. 67.

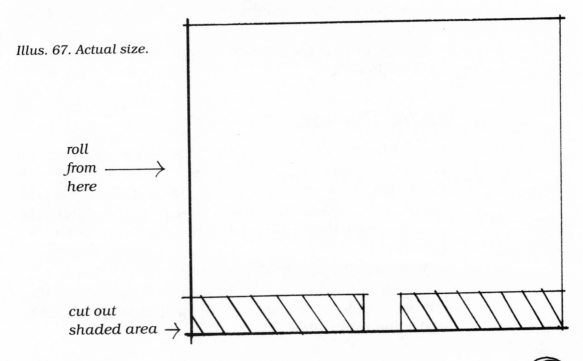

Illus. 67. Actual size.

roll from here →

cut out shaded area →

Roll the turkey caller around a pencil beginning from the narrow side. Now slide the tube off the pencil and either hold the roll tight or put a piece of tape around it.

Finally, fold the little flap down so it covers the hole at the end of the tube, as shown in Illus. 68. Your turkey caller is ready for use.

To use the turkey caller, you can either blow or suck air through it. Put the open end in your mouth and suck air back through it. If it doesn't make a strange sound, do it either softer or a bit harder. Draw in short breaths and see what happens to the tone.

Now turn the turkey caller around and put the flap end into the middle of your mouth. Make sure that the flap end doesn't touch any part of your mouth. (Warning! Don't slobber! You don't want people to think you are a turkey!) Blow gently. Blow harder. Blow in little bursts of air. In just

flap ↓

Illus. 68

a few seconds you will discover which tone you like best. Cup your hands around the turkey caller and then open and close them as you blow to vary the sounds. Just don't blow so hard that the little flap cannot vibrate.

Try making turkey callers which are longer or shorter than your first one. Experiment with different kinds of paper. Make flaps larger or smaller. Just make certain the flap is large enough to completely cover the open end of the caller.

Try this one on the playground and watch all the turkeys flock to you!

Comb Hummer

A pocket comb and a piece of paper are all that are needed to make a comb hummer. Thin paper such as tissue paper or waxed paper generally makes the best sound. Cut a piece of it which is a little larger than the distance from the tips of the comb's teeth to the back of the comb.

With your fingers, hold the paper tightly at the ends of the comb. Place the teeth of the comb in front of your lips, but not so close that it touches them. The paper should be under the comb (Illus. 69).

Illus. 69

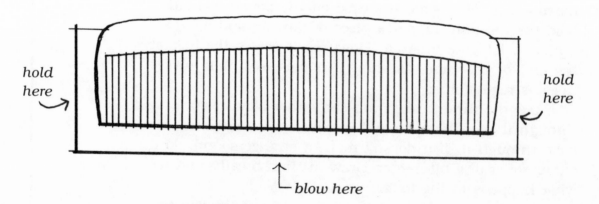

hold
here

hold
here

blow here

Begin blowing and humming at the same time towards the ends of the teeth and the edge of the paper. Direct the stream of air along the length of the comb. Hold the paper tightly in place. When you get just the right amount of air flowing at just the right speed, the paper will begin to vibrate. By changing the distance from the comb to your mouth and by humming louder or softer, you can make interesting sounds with your comb hummer.

You realize this is not great music.

It's easier than playing the violin. Just don't ask to use my comb.

Wind Woofer

Wind woofers were made by pioneer children as fun toys. Some say the American Indians also made a type of wind woofer as well.

A wind woofer is made from a piece of thin wood about 12 inches long and 1½ or so inches wide. It does not have to be exactly this size but should be close. Your wind woofer should not be more than ¼ inch thick. It may work better if it is a bit thinner.

Illus. 70

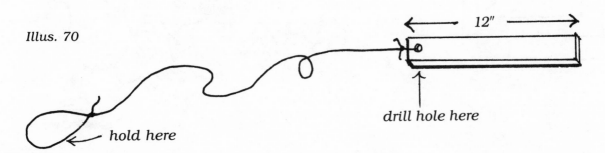

hold here

12"

drill hole here

Ask someone to drill or bore a hole about an inch from one end, as shown in Illus. 70. Cut a piece of nylon or very strong cord about 4 feet long. Lightweight or thin cords will break when you start spinning the wind woofer. Tie one end with a *firm* knot through the hole in the wind woofer. Tie a loop in the other end of the cord to hold it. Make sure your knots are tight. You are now ready to create sounds.

Hold onto the loop and begin to spin the wind woofer rapidly above your head. Don't do this inside unless you have an entire gym in which to spin the wind woofer. You need plenty of space to use this terrific noisemaker.

The faster the woofer spins the better the sound it makes. It will begin with a woofing and shuffing sound. If you can spin it fast enough, it will sound like a growl or even a roar.

Try making woofers thicker or thinner, wider or narrower. If you have sandpaper handy, make the edges thinner. This makes the woofer move more easily through the air and changes its tone.

Remember to check the cord and knots before each spin.

Don't let go of it unless you want to pay for a broken window.

Can Clompers

Can clompers have absolutely no social value. But they make great noise on sidewalks. So let's make a pair or two.

Begin with two steel cans (not aluminum!). With a hammer and nail, carefully make two holes in each can. Make these holes directly across from each other and just below the rim of each can.

You need two strong strings or cords about 5 feet long. Tie both ends of each cord into the holes of each can. Make the knots good and tight. As soon as you have tied four knots in the ends of four cords, as shown in Illus. 71, your clompers are ready to use.

Carefully place your feet on top of each can clomper so the strings are on either side of each foot. Hold the strings in each hand and pull up just enough to keep the can tight against the bottom of your shoe.

Take a step, making sure to hold the can in place by pulling up on the cords. Take another step and then another. With just a little practice, you are ready to go for a walk on your clompers. You will certainly get lots of attention!

A second type of can clomper is easier to make. For this kind, you need two empty condensed-milk cans. These are the kind which have been opened just by poking two small holes in the top.

Place the can on its side on the ground or sidewalk. Now quickly stamp your foot down hard on the center of the can. The two ends should crunch over and lock tight on both sides of the sole of your shoe, as shown in Illus. 72.

Illus. 71

Illus. 72

Stamp the second can onto your other foot and you are ready for a stroll.

If a can clomper begins to loosen, you can usually just stamp down hard and tighten it. Aluminum beverage cans will also work for the second type of clompers. Some are made so thin that they may not cling very well to your shoes. Try them and see.

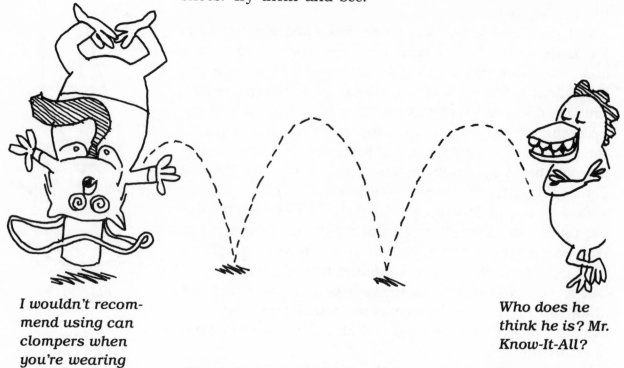

I wouldn't recommend using can clompers when you're wearing sandals.

Who does he think he is? Mr. Know-It-All?

Bicycle Flappers

With a clothespin and a playing card, you can turn your bicycle into a fantastic noisemaker. If you use two clothespins and playing cards, you can make twice the noise.

Use the clothespin to clip a playing card into the front-wheel fork of your bicycle. Adjust it so that only the edge of the card touches the spokes as the wheel revolves. See Illus. 73 for the right position. *Warning: Make absolutely certain the clothespin doesn't get in the path of the spokes.* If the clothespin gets twisted inside, it could ruin your spokes.

As the wheel turns, the edge of the playing card hits the spokes—creating a wonderful sound. The faster the wheel revolves the better the sound.

Don't use brand-new playing cards, since they can get

ruined rather quickly. Once you have used up half a deck of playing cards and filled the neighborhood with all the rattle and flapping people can stand, it is time to move on to another type of spoke noisemaker.

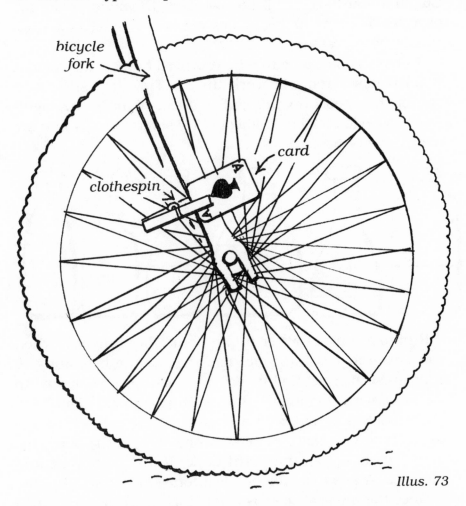

Illus. 73

Inflate a balloon only part way and tie the open end shut. Push the air into the opposite end and wrap the knotted end of the balloon around the front fork of your bike. Clamp it with a clothespin. Be sure the balloon is in front of the fork, not behind it.

Begin to ride slowly. Then speed up a bit. The sound the balloon makes is very much like that of an extremely noisy motor. Experiment until you learn just how much air to put into the balloon. Don't inflate it very full. If you do, the balloon will last about five seconds. All it takes is too much speed or a rough spot on the spokes to break the balloon. But the popping and roaring sound is great while it lasts.

Musical Bottles

If you have eight bottles and the desire to create some really interesting sounds, you can make a musical scale. But first you have to fill the bottles with varying amounts of water. It helps if the bottles are pretty much alike but this is not necessary.

To make good bottle music, you need a wooden striker. A wooden dowel rod will work fine. A Tinkertoy stick with one of the spools on the end is great. Actually, any light-weight wooden striker will work. Try several things and see which works best.

Run just a bit of water into a bottle. Tap it lightly. When you create a pleasing tone, use that as the beginning of your musical scale. Call it "do" and then work your way up the scale with the other bottles with re, mi, etc. (Illus. 74).

The trick is to add a bit more water to each bottle in line to create a tone exactly one step higher than the bottle before. This is not all that hard to do. It just takes time and patience. A good ear for musical tone won't hurt either.

Once the musical scale is created, tap each bottle in turn and play your way from do up to do. Try to play "Mary Had a Little Lamb," "Twinkle, Twinkle Little Star," or any other song that you wish.

If you can't leave your musical bottles with water in them and want to use them again, here's a hint to save you time. Put a little piece of tape on each bottle to show where the water level should be when you refill that bottle. You will have to do a bit of tuning, but all musicians tune up before playing.

Here's another hint. Don't strike the bottles too hard. A carpet flooded with water takes a lot of fun out of a concert.

Illus. 74

60

Tin-Pan Band

Anyone can make all sorts of "music" with a tin-pan band. If you have ever been lucky enough to travel to the Bahamas, you have most likely heard the steel bands which entertain there. They use specially made oversized tin pans and steel drums which can play any musical note.

Don't use your family's cooking pans and kettles, no matter how great they may sound. And stay away from pans or pots which have an enamelled coating which is likely to flake off into sharp little pieces. Ask your parent for any old pots or pans that you can use (Illus. 75).

Try scraping, striking, and rattling any empty container or can for your rhythm band. The variety of sounds you can create will astound you.

When you and your friends have your band assembled, the neighbors will be the first to know. Some will probably call on the telephone. Others may come over or shout at you. What you do then is up to you.

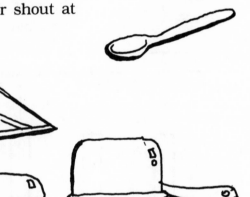

Illus. 75

Don't tell anyone where you got the idea for this.

Tell your folks that Owl made you do it.

Wind Chimes

Wind chimes make pleasant sounds that nearly everyone enjoys hearing. A wind chime is nothing more than a number of objects hanging by thread or thin wire. There may be as few as three hanging objects or as many as ten. It is best to use nylon thread to hang wind chimes indoors. Thin wire is better for those on a porch or other outside area.

To construct your own set of wind chimes, you need either a strip of metal, a stick of wood, or another material that you can make into a circle, and however many hanging chimes you decide to use. Then it is all a matter of placing the chimes so they strike each other in a breeze and make pleasant sounds.

What makes good wind chimes? Any piece of metal or other hard material which will make a nice sound when the wind blows them together. Strips or rectangles of some hard plastics make good wind chimes. You can make a

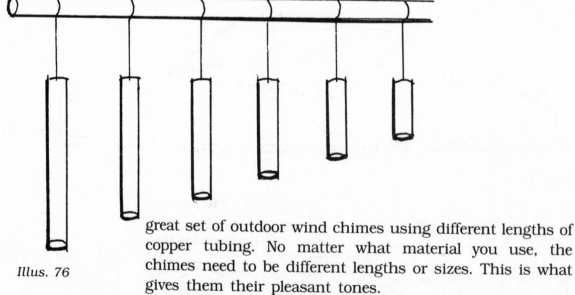

Illus. 76

great set of outdoor wind chimes using different lengths of copper tubing. No matter what material you use, the chimes need to be different lengths or sizes. This is what gives them their pleasant tones.

If the materials for your chimes are metal or plastic, you will probably need a drill to make the holes by which the chimes hang. Ask an adult to do this for you. Before going to all the trouble of making the holes and hanging the chimes, check them for tone first. Lightly strike two chimes together. If they make a good sound, go on with the project. If not, look for other materials.

The easiest way to set up wind chimes is in a straight line. Chimes made from metal tubing might look like Illus. 76.

Test the spacing between the chimes by gently shaking the set before hanging it. The idea is to have the various chimes close enough to strike each other but not so close that the wires or strings become tangled.

A circular set of wind chimes is a bit harder to make, but it usually works better than a straight set. The biggest problem is finding a round hanger. One solution is to make one out of heavy wire—a stiff coat hanger will work. Space the chimes so they strike each other in even a gentle breeze. A completed set might look like Illus. 77.

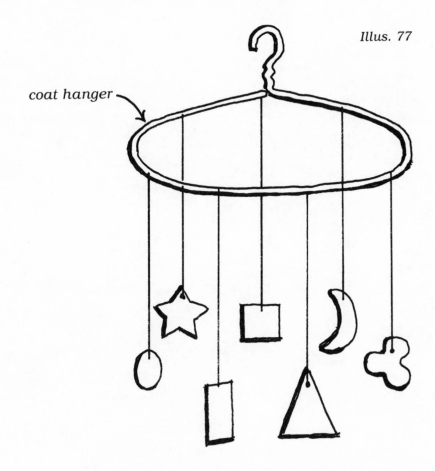

Illus. 77

coat hanger

One person made a fantastic set of wind chimes using tiny bottles of various sizes. This was strictly an indoor set since the glass would likely break in a strong breeze.

•5•
Terrific Toys

Boomerang

You don't have to live in Australia in order to make a little boomerang which really works. All it takes is a 3-inch square of cardboard. File cards, manila folders, or cereal boxes work just fine.

Cut out a boomerang which looks about like the one shown in Illus. 78. Don't worry about making it exactly like the illustration. Just come as close as possible. It will work.

To fly your boomerang, place it on top of your closed hand, as shown in Illus. 79. Flick end A with your other forefinger. Be sure to snap fast and hard. The best way to do this is to hold the end of your forefinger against the middle of your thumb. Then just relax the thumb and snap your forefinger forward. When it strikes your boomerang that is all there is to it.

After you have practiced a few times, the boomerang should come whirling back to you every time.

Try making other boomerangs a little larger or a bit smaller than your first one. You might want to experiment by making one arm a little longer than the other. This will change the way the boomerang flies.

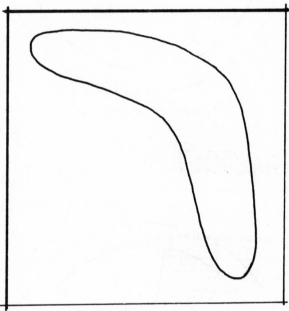
Illus. 78. Actual size.

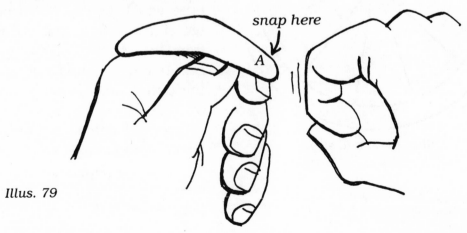
Illus. 79

Illus. 80. Actual size.

Illus. 81. Actual size.

Breeze Ball

To contruct a breeze ball, you need a compass, a good pair of scissors, a ruler, a pencil, and a small piece of notebook paper.

Begin by drawing a circle about 3 inches across. Then set the compass legs ¼ inch smaller and draw another circle inside the first. *Do not* change the compass distance for the next step.

Put the point of the compass on the smaller circle at any point. Make a mark with the compass pencil on that circle. Now put the point in the mark you just made. Make another mark on the circle. Keep doing this until you have gone all the way around the inner circle. There should be six marks, as shown in Illus. 80.

Now connect the compass marks which are opposite each other by drawing straight lines between them.

Next draw three more lines dividing the six sections you just made in half. Space these lines exactly between the lines you just drew. It should look like Illus. 81.

Very carefully cut each of the twelve lines which extend out from the center of the circle. Make the first cut from the center. Don't tear the paper. *Do not* cut out the circle yet. Just cut the twelve lines coming out from the center.

Start anywhere and fold one of the triangular sections so it is at a right angle to the paper. Crease it. Fold the next one in the exact opposite direction. Crease it. Alternate folds until you work your way around the circle. Six triangles should stick out in one direction and six in the other.

Now cut out the outer circle. Your breeze ball is ready to use. It should look like Illus. 82.

Drop the breeze ball on the ground where a breeze can reach it and watch it take off across the playground. With just a small bit of wind, a breeze ball will travel faster than you might expect.

Experiment with various sizes of breeze balls. Make them from different colors of construction paper to see which works best.

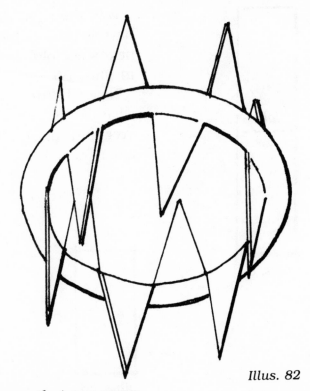

Illus. 82

Finger Flapper

A finger flapper is just a little fold of paper that you move with your thumb and forefinger to look like a mouth. To make a finger flapper, start with an 8½-inch square piece of notebook paper.

Fold the paper in half. Open it and fold each side so the edges meet at the middle crease (Illus. 83). The paper should look like Illus. 84.

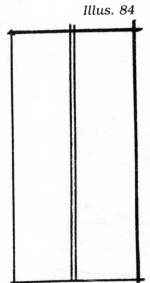

Illus. 84

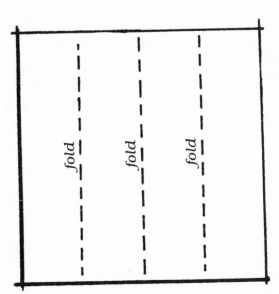

fold   fold   fold

Illus. 83

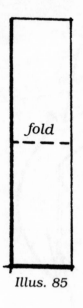

fold

Illus. 85

Fold the right side over the left so that you have a long, narrow strip of folded paper, as shown in Illus. 85. For the next step, fold the bottom of the narrow strip up to the top in Illus. 86.

Now fold the top four layers of paper down to the bottom edge of the paper, as shown in Illus. 87. Turn the paper over and fold the other four layers down to the bottom—Illus. 88.

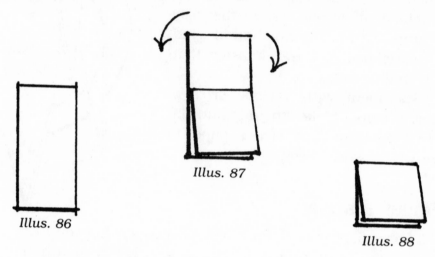

Illus. 87

Illus. 86

Illus. 88

Place the folded finger flapper on your desk and let it open up. It looks like the letter "W" on its side. If you look at the top and bottom layers, you will see two little pockets. One is at the very top. The other is at the bottom. It should look like Illus. 89.

Slip your forefinger into the top pocket. Then put your thumb into the bottom pocket. When you move your finger and thumb, your finger flapper moves like a mouth. If you want to, draw eyes and a nose on the top and a tongue inside the mouth. Move the finger flapper as you speak and let it say what it wants to.

Illus. 89

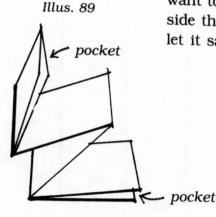

pocket

pocket

Wait a minute. It can say almost *anything it wants to.*

Just so it doesn't say, "Who . . . who . . . whooo!"

Ball Toss

In one form or another, this game has been played all over the world for many years.

First roll a sheet of notebook paper into a cone. Keep one end tight and let the other end spread out so the opening is about 4 inches across. Tape or staple the loose edge to keep the cone from unravelling.

Wad a 4-inch square of paper into a tight little ball about an inch across. Wrap a strip or two of tape around it to keep it tight.

Make a hole in one side of the open end of the cone. This hole should be down an inch or so from the top. Cut a piece of string or thread about 3 feet long. Tie one end into the hole you just made in the cone. Tie or tape the other end to the ball (Illus. 90).

Now to test your skill. Hold the cone in one hand and toss the ball up with the other. Catch the ball in the cone. If you miss, toss the ball up again. It should always go as high as the string allows. After you catch it, use the cone to toss the ball for the next catch.

Try to catch ten in a row. Then go for twenty. When you are able to do that, make a new cone with its open end a bit smaller than the one you just made. Then start going for records with the new cone.

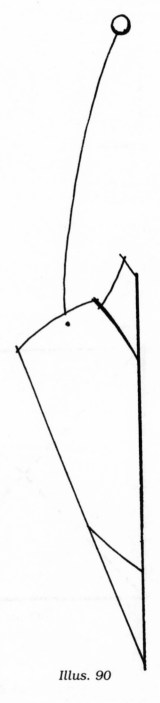

Illus. 90

A variation of this is the ring catcher. Make a tight paper cone or even a tightly rolled cylinder of paper. Use the cone with the *pointed* end up. Tie a wooden or plastic ring to the pointed end. Now try to catch the ring on the cone's pointed end.

This version is quite a bit more difficult than catching the ball in the cone, but it is a very good contest. Challenge others or just go for your own records.

The smaller the ring, the better the game.

Cootie Catcher

The cootie catcher is an old favorite, and it's easy to make and fun to play with. If you use it to pinch necks and ears or grab at others, it may just get you into some trouble.

Start with an 8½-inch square of paper. Notebook paper is perfect. Make the two diagonal folds as shown in Illus. 91. Unfold the paper. Then fold the four corners into the middle. Crease these folds and do not unfold them. Your cootie catcher should look like Illus. 92.

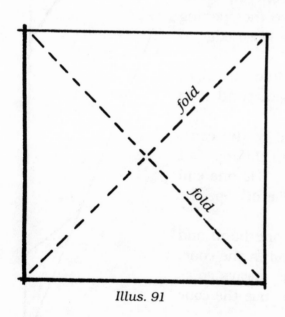

Illus. 91

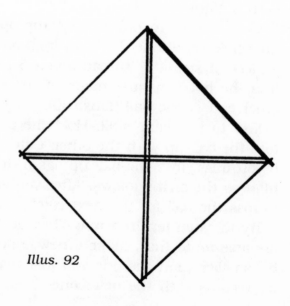

Illus. 92

Turn the paper over. Fold each corner into the middle. Crease these folds and do not unfold the paper, as shown in Illus. 93.

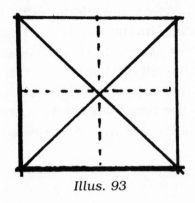

Illus. 93

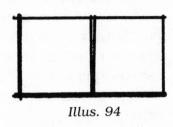

Illus. 94

Your next step is to fold the right side over to the left side. Crease this fold carefully. Now unfold the paper.

Now fold the top side to the bottom and crease firmly. Do not unfold the paper. The cootie catcher should now look like Illus. 94.

Take hold of the two sides at the bottom corners, using both hands. Slowly push your hands together. The four corners of the paper should begin to spread apart. If necessary, hold the paper with one hand and spread out the four corners with the other.

Your cootie catcher should look like Illus. 95. Slip your thumb and three fingers of one hand into the four corners. By moving your fingers back and forth and opening and

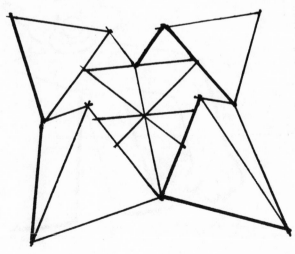

Illus. 95

shutting them, your cootie catcher should open in either direction.

The cootie catcher is great for picking up items or just pinching your friends. Some players write "yes" and "no" inside the catcher and use it to answer questions. Others number the various inside panels. On the backs of these panels they write different words or answers. This becomes a fortune-telling cootie catcher. To tell someone's fortune, ask the person to choose a number. Open and close the catcher a number of times until the panel with the chosen number appears. Then lift the panel and the "fortune" appears!

Tightrope Walker

Gymnasts *wish* they had perfect balance. Circus performers *have* to have perfect balance. The little fellow shown here will balance without any problems. Trace the pattern in Illus. 96 on stiff paper or a file card and then cut it out. Don't worry about making the figure perfect—it will balance anyway. Start with a figure about 3 inches high. Later on you may want to make one larger or smaller.

Illus. 96. Actual size.

Now you need a piece of thread or very thin string about 2 or 3 feet long. Get someone to hold it for you or tie one end to a hook or chair or anything available.

Set your little paper figure on the string so it is between his legs. He should balance fine. Give him a load to carry by putting a paper clip onto the end of each arm. He should balance even better than before.

Blow gently and your little acrobat will slip along the thread without ever losing his balance.

Make several acrobats of different sizes. Draw faces on them and color them if you wish. Just make certain to give them long legs and long arms which hang down at their sides.

Try hooking several clips onto each arm. Challenge friends to make their own balancing acrobats. Just one thing. Don't blow on the tightrope walker from either side. That's the one thing that may cause him to lose his balance and fall from the high wire.

For even greater performances, use paper clips to lengthen each arm by attaching a drinking straw to each one. Point the straw arms downwards. Now put your acrobat on his high wire and see how he performs.

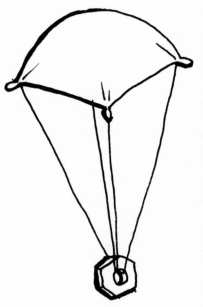

Parachutes

It takes about five minutes to make a parachute. Once it is finished, it will last as long as you want to use it. About the only thing that can go wrong is if you get it stuck in a tree branch. If that happens, just make a new parachute.

Begin with a piece of cloth which is square or nearly so. Size does not matter all that much. Make one 15–18 inches across for your first effort.

Cut four pieces of string the same length. Make the strings about as long as your cloth is wide. Tie one string to each corner of the cloth. Then run the loose ends of the strings through a heavy nut from a bolt, or some metal washers, or anything which is fairly heavy and can be tied to the ends of the string (Illus. 97).

Once the weight is tied tightly, wad the cloth into your hand, and get ready to throw it as high as possible into

Illus. 97

the air. Don't wrap the strings around the cloth or else the parachute won't open properly.

Find an open space and give your parachute a high throw. It should open and float to earth. Experiment with the way you wad or fold it to find the best way to have it open quickly. Try different sizes of cloth and different lengths of string. Add more weight or make it lighter. Each change will make the parachute act differently.

Throw your parachute up into open spaces. Stay away from trees and power lines. Who wants to have to make a new parachute every five minutes?

Impossible Swinging Pencil

All you need for this amazing stunt is a wooden pencil with an eraser and a paper clip.

Straighten the paper clip and then bend it so that it looks about like the one in Illus. 98. Don't worry about getting it exactly right. You can adjust the bends without any problem.

Carefully stick one end of the clip into the pencil's eraser, as shown in Illus. 98, and you are ready to test your impossible swinging pencil.

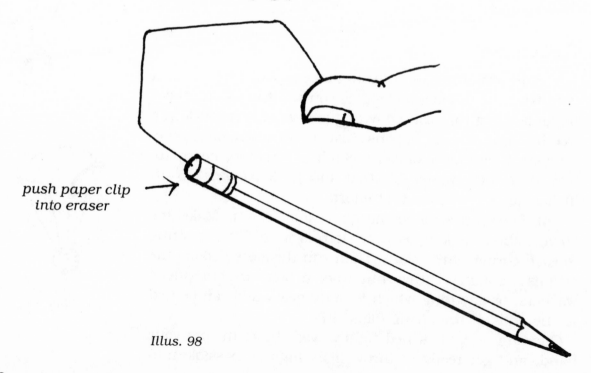

push paper clip
into eraser

Illus. 98

Place the end of the bent paper clip on the tip of your finger. Let go of the pencil. If you have the clip shaped correctly, the pencil should swing under your finger. It should not fall off. If it does, change the angle of the bends in the clip and try again. Once you have the hang of it, try changing the angles in the bent clip. It is possible to cause the pencil to hang differently and move in many directions.

Look for other places to hang your swinging pencil. Unless a surface is too slick, it will hang almost anywhere it has room to swing.

I hope your teacher is really into this sort of thing.

There's only one way to find out.

•6•
Party Tricks and Tokens

Flying Fold

This little trick does not really fly. The flying part is just to keep others from seeing what you do to make it work. Most people never will figure out how it works until you show them.

Cut out a piece of fairly stiff paper or an index card about 2 × 4½ inches. Fold it as shown in Illus. 99. Fold A towards you. Fold B away from you. Fold C towards you.

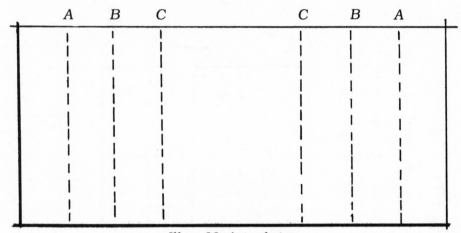

Illus. 99. Actual size.

Crease each fold carefully. Do this at both ends so you have two small accordion folds. Now push the folds down so the paper looks like Illus. 100. While it is flat, fold it over— away from you—and crease it as shown in Illus. 101.

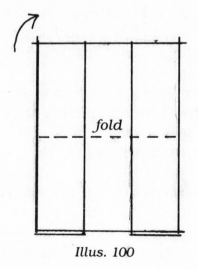

Illus. 100

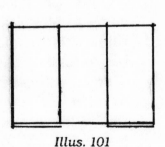

Illus. 101

Unfold the paper or card and hold it so it is flat. Dare someone to touch it with just their thumb and forefinger and refold it so it looks like Illus. 101. The person may not touch the paper with any other part of his body, with another object, nor may another person touch it.

The dare is pretty safe unless someone stumbles onto the solution by accident. When it is your turn to prove it can be done, hold the paper between your thumb and forefinger, as shown in Illus. 102.

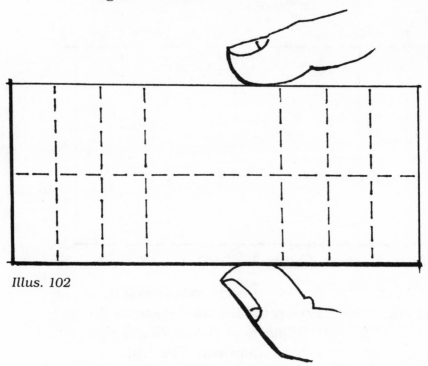

Illus. 102

Gently tighten your thumb and forefinger towards each other. Just like magic, the folds should begin to fall into place. Folds C will be followed by folds B and finally folds A. It's as simple as that.

In order to keep others from realizing exactly how you perform the trick, move your hand as though you were going to slowly launch a paper glider. This makes others think it is the slow-flying movement which causes the paper to fold.

Practice this several times before you attempt to show it to others. If you have trouble, make certain that you fold the middle crease slightly with your thumb and forefinger just before you begin the trick. Then it's just a matter of confusing everyone with your flying fold!

Paper Puffer

A paper puffer is lots of fun at a party. You can make one in about two minutes. It will come unrolling out of your mouth fast enough to startle all your friends.

A sheet of notebook paper will work. Tissue or tracing paper is better if you have it. Place the paper in front of you on a table with the 11-inch side towards you (Illus. 103). Make a fold about 1 inch wide. Then just keep folding the paper over and over so you end up with a strip 1 inch wide and as long as the paper, as shown in Illus. 104.

Fold one end of this long strip about ⅛ inch and crease it firmly. Then just roll the strip up around that fold. Stop when you are 2 inches from the other end. Squeeze the roll tightly and hold it in place a few seconds.

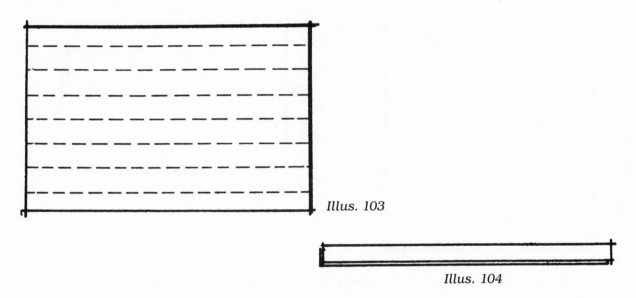

Illus. 103

Illus. 104

Make sure the unrolled end forms a hollow tube for you to blow into as shown in Illus. 105. Place that end to your lips, let go of the rolled part of the puffer, and blow. It will instantly unroll and extend straight out. Reroll it and do it again and again.

Experiment with paper longer and narrower than notebook paper. Try a piece 16–18 inches long and only 6 inches wide. Thin paper will vibrate as you blow and make an interesting sound.

Glue a very tiny plastic whistle into the end of your puffer. When it unrolls, it whistles at the same time!

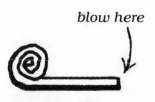

blow here

Illus. 105

Party Hat

This paper hat doesn't make noise or fly. But it's perfect to wear at a party. Besides, once you make one, everyone will want a hat of his or her own.

Begin with a rectangular piece of paper about 12 × 18 inches or even a little larger. A piece of newspaper makes a terrific hat.

Fold the paper exactly in half from top to bottom (Illus. 106).

Now determine the exact middle of the fold (Point A in Illus. 107). The easiest way to do this is to double the pa-

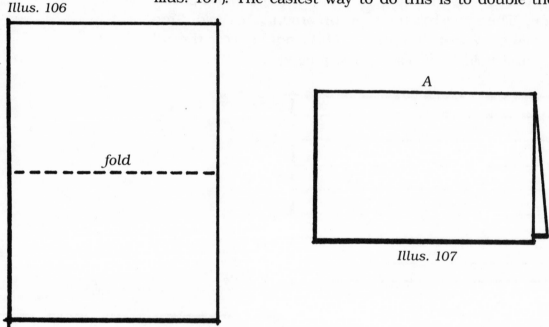

Illus. 106

fold

A

Illus. 107

per along the fold and put a little crease in the middle to mark it.

As shown in Illus. 108, fold down corner B and crease it.

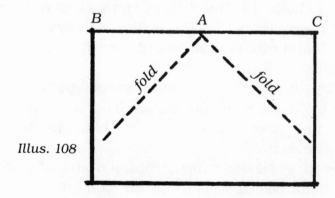

B   *A*   *C*

fold   *fold*

Illus. 108

84

Do the same for corner C. Illus. 109 shows what your hat should look like after these folds.

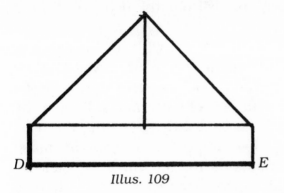

Illus. 109

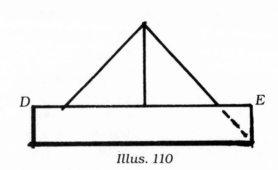

Illus. 110

Fold up one of the bottom DE strips (Illus. 110). Turn the hat over and fold up the other bottom strip in the same way. It should now look like Illus. 110.

To finish your party hat, fold corners D and E over and crease them sharply. Then open your hat and slip it onto your head. It should look like the hat in Illus. 111. Since party hats are so easy to make, try using larger or smaller paper to get the perfect fit.

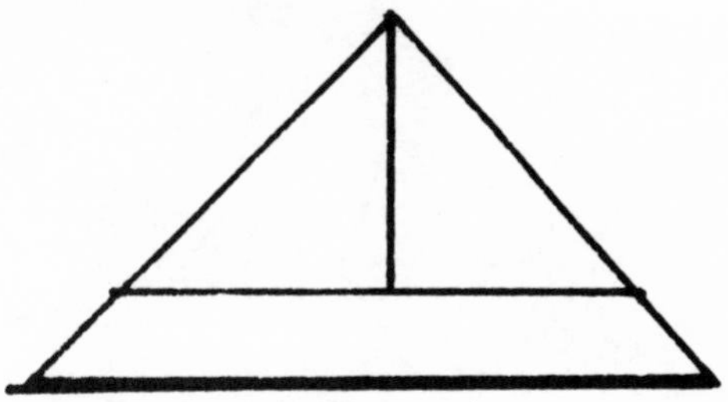

Illus. 111

Balloon Times Three

An ordinary balloon makes three great noisemakers. One of these is a flying type, which is an extra bonus.

Blow up a balloon and let go of it. As it flies around the room it makes a noise as the balloon darts and dashes about until it runs out of air. Blow it up and do it again. This is a great way to entertain small children if you want to get their attention.

Now blow up the balloon and hold the mouth closed so the air will not escape. With your other hand, begin to rub the tight balloon with the tips of your fingers. Draw your fingers along the balloon's surface. Move them in a twisting motion. Once you get the hang of it, you can create sounds which are guaranteed to attract attention. Try this in the library and you will find yourself out the door in nothing flat!

A third way to make great sounds with an inflated balloon is by letting just a little air escape while you hold it. After blowing up your balloon, hold the neck tightly closed with the thumbs and forefingers of both hands. Loosen the pressure so just a little air escapes. By stretching the neck of the balloon tight and loosening it a bit, you can make fantastic squeaks and howls as the air leaves the balloon.

All good balloons end in the same way. Eventually they break. Then it's time to blow up another one.

Your friends may get tired of hearing you make so many noises with balloons.

I'm already tired of listening to you.

Soap Bubbles

Soap bubbles are easy to make and lots of fun. Some are big while others are quite small. When a little breeze blows, soap bubbles float quite a distance before they strike something and burst.

First, you need a spool with no thread on it. It does not matter whether the spool is wooden or plastic or even Styrofoam. Just choose a spool with a fairly small hole in the middle. If the hole is too large, you can only blow big bubbles and they can be hard to get started.

To mix your bubble material, use a shallow dish or a saucer. A soft cake of soap such as Ivory makes good bubbles—and so do most dishwashing liquids.

Rub a cake of soap into just a little water until the liquid becomes extremely thick with dissolved soap. If you use dishwashing liquid, mix a little water with it but not too much.

Dip one end of the spool into the soap mixture (Illus. 112). You don't have to cover the spool—that will only make a mess. Lift the spool and put the dry end to your lips. Blow gently. A soap bubble should begin to form at the other end of the spool. If the liquid dribbles off or a bubble quickly bursts, it means your liquid has too much water and not enough soap.

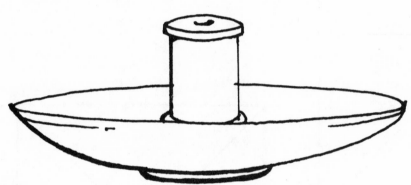

Illus. 112

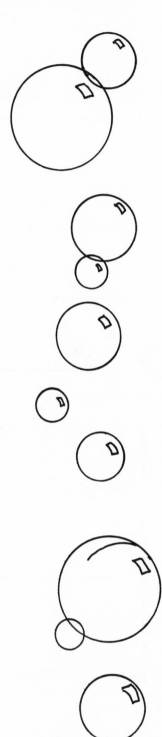

With just a little practice, you will learn how to make a single large bubble or a whole series of little ones. Blow directly into the center of the spool or tip it so you blow at an angle to make different sizes. Blow slowly to make large bubbles. Blow faster to make a chain of little bubbles.

Stand near an air vent or other breeze and let it carry your bubbles across the room. When you are outside the breezes will take your soap bubbles with them.

There is just one thing you need to keep in mind. These bubbles are made out of soap. When a bubble lands or strikes an object it breaks, leaving a little ring of moist soap. Unless you want to spend lots of time cleaning up, don't let your bubbles hit anything which will be hurt by the little circle of moisture and soap.

Hop Toad

This jumping creature is folded out of stiff paper or file cards. Start with a piece about 4 × 6 or 5 × 8 inches. As shown in Illus. 113, fold each side diagonally to the opposite edge. Crease each fold firmly before unfolding the paper.

Next fold the top of the paper down to make fold AB, as shown in Illus. 114. Crease this fold firmly, then unfold it.

Now take hold of point A with one hand and point B with the other. Bring your hands together carefully. This forces A and B towards each other. The folds you have

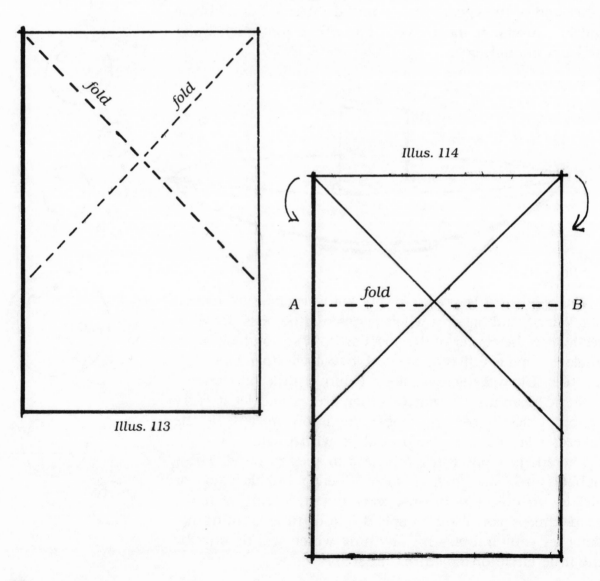

Illus. 114

Illus. 113

creased into place allow the card to fold inward on itself, forming the triangle shown in Illus. 115. Crease this triangle firmly.

Fold the top layer of point C to point E. Then fold point D to E (Illus. 116). (Each side you fold up consists of two

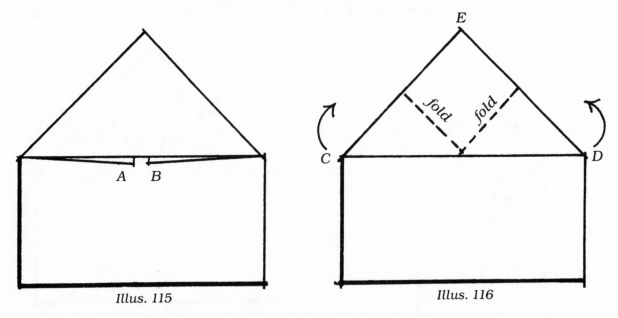

Illus. 115   Illus. 116

layers of paper.) Crease these folds firmly and do not unfold them. Your card should look like Illus. 117.

Now fold point C towards you, as shown in Illus. 118,

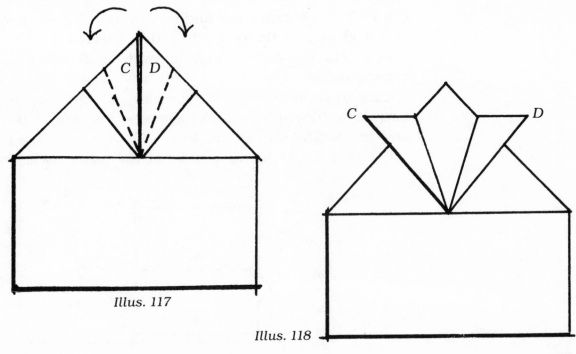

Illus. 117

Illus. 118

and crease it. Do the same for point D. Your hop toad has just grown its front legs (Illus. 118), and is almost ready to make its first practice hop.

Make the two side folds, as shown in Illus. 119. Crease these folds and do not unfold them.

Fold the head towards you, as shown in Illus. 120.

Illus. 119

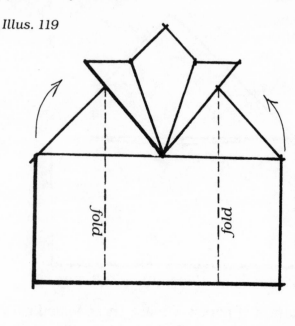

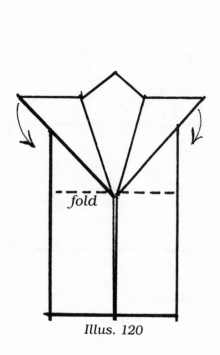

Illus. 120

Crease it firmly into place and do not unfold it. Turn your hop toad over so the pointed head is towards you.

Now fold the bottom end upwards and crease it, as shown in Illus. 121.

Congratulations! You have just formed your hop toad's back legs. Turn the toad over again so his head is on top and he's sitting on his rear legs.

Put your finger in the middle of the toad's back. Press

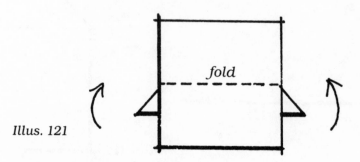

Illus. 121

his rear legs down as you slide your finger down his back. The instant your finger slips off the toad he will take a quick hop. If your toad flips over on his head, put a few paper clips on his feet to add some weight.

Experiment with different kinds of paper or file cards. Make hop toads with longer bodies which will give them longer back legs. Challenge your friends to a contest to see whose hop toad hops the greatest distance.

Magic Finger Trap

Some people say the Chinese invented the paper finger trap. This may be so. Others suspect it was first made by an eleven-year-old student who was tired of doing homework. This probably is not true but it makes a good story.

Cut out a piece of a heavy-duty grocery bag that is 6 inches wide and 16–18 inches long. One of those big bags has enough paper for at least half a dozen finger traps.

Cut two 12–14-inch slits in the paper about 2½ inches from each side edge, as shown in Illus. 122.

Illus. 122

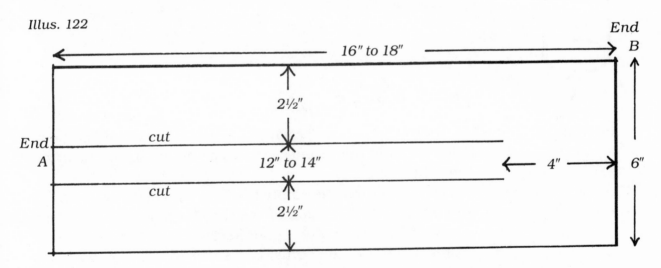

To roll up your finger trap, first put a book or paperweight on end B to hold it in place, or have a friend hold it. Use a pencil to help make a tight roll beginning at end A of the three tabs. Make sure each of the three strips rolls evenly. Don't get upset if you have to start once or twice. (It took a couple of experts five times to get it rolled right!)

Once you have rolled all the way to end B, *carefully* allow the rolled paper to slip open just a little bit. The pencil will drop out of the roll. Let the roll continue to open until the hole is just large enough so you can slip a finger into the roll. It should be a very snug fit, but not so tight that your finger won't go all the way into the roll.

Now tape the roll so it won't open any more with cellophane or masking tape. Use three pieces about an inch long—one piece at each end and the third one around the middle. Your trap is ready (Illus. 123).

Slip one finger of each hand into opposite ends of the trap. Make sure they go all the way into it. Now try to pull your fingers out without tearing the trap. If your trap is made correctly, you will find both fingers firmly held inside.

Try this yourself a few times before using it on a friend. There is not any danger to this trap. It is easy to remove the tape or simply rip the trap open. Since the challenge is to pull free without tearing the paper, it is loads of fun.

Don't use the finger trap with small children who may get frightened. Make sure they know it's just a game and won't hurt them.

insert finger

Illus. 123

Soap-Bottle Surprise

Did you ever wonder what to do with the plastic bottle of dishwashing liquid after the soap was all gone? Read on and find out.

First wash out the empty bottle to get rid of any soap left in it. Look at the *inside* of the cap. There is probably some sort of plastic stopper that keeps too much soap from squirting out of the bottle. Use a pair of pliers to twist this out and throw it away. *Do not* pull out the little plunger which goes upwards and downwards to keep the bottle from shooting out soap. *Do not* use a knife to remove the little plastic plug. If necessary, get an adult to help you.

All you now need is a piece of string 2 feet long. Tie a knot in one end of it. Be sure the knot is large enough so that it is bigger than the center hole in the little plunger valve. Screw the lid back onto the bottle.

Thread the string through the plunger and into the bottle so that just the knot shows. It should look like Illus. 124.

Now for the big surprise. Give the plastic container a fast squeeze. The string will come squirting out of the bottle because of the air pressure behind the knot. The person will think he is being squirted with dishwashing liquid. Use a red string and it will look like ketchup.

Illus. 124

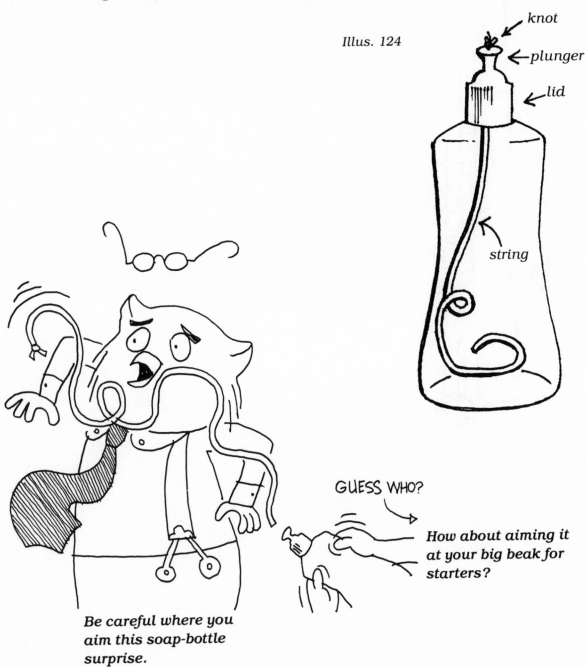

knot

←plunger

←lid

string

GUESS WHO?

How about aiming it at your big beak for starters?

Be careful where you aim this soap-bottle surprise.

Clothespin Flipper

The easiest way to make a clothespin flipper is to fasten a bottle cap to a clothespin, as shown in Illus. 125. Wrap a piece of masking tape around one side of the clothespin to hold the cap in place. Just fold the ends of the tape over the sides of the lid and press the tape down firmly.

Wad up a little piece of paper and place it in the bottle cap. Put the clothespin on a table and press down on the end with the bottle cap. Then let it go. Your clothespin flipper will send the ball of paper into the air.

This flipper doesn't fire things very far, but it is fun to make and use. Try sending other objects into the air.

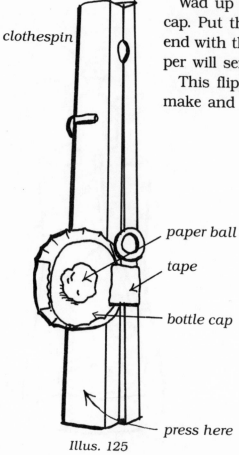

clothespin

paper ball

tape

bottle cap

press here

Illus. 125

•7•
Super Spinners

Pinwheel

People have been making pinwheels for about as long as paper and pins have been around.

Start with a piece of paper which is 6 inches square. It must be square or the completed pinwheel will be off balance.

Find the middle point by drawing diagonal lines from corner 1 to corner 3 and another from 2 to 4, as shown in Illus. 126. Where the two lines cross is the exact middle of the square of paper.

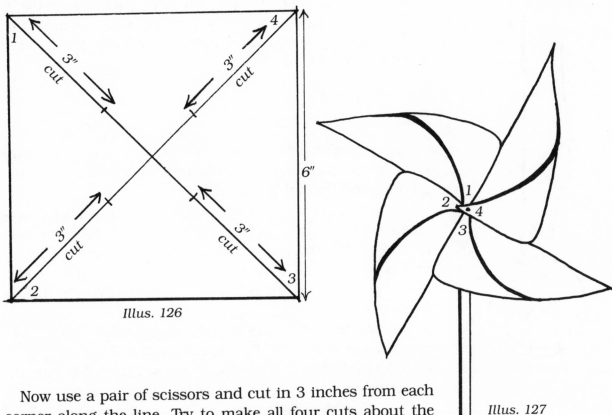

Illus. 126

Illus. 127

Now use a pair of scissors and cut in 3 inches from each corner along the line. Try to make all four cuts about the same length but don't worry if you are off a little.

Now comes the tricky part. Bend corners 1, 2, 3, and 4 into the middle so their tips overlap slightly. Do not fold and crease the corners—just bend them inward. Look carefully at Illus. 127. The numbered corners are all on a particular side. You *must* bend only these corners, not the unnumbered ones. As soon as you finish, look at your pinwheel and see whether you bent the wrong corners.

Push a straight pin through the four bent-in corners and

through the middle of the pinwheel. The pin's head is at the front of the pinwheel. Now push the pin into one end of a plastic drinking straw and your pinwheel is ready to whirl.

Blow on the pinwheel and it should whirl. Wave it through the air and it will spin faster. Hold it up in a breeze or in front of a fan and it will turn rapidly.

Now that you see how to make a pinwheel, it is time to experiment. Use different sorts of paper and see which works best. Color your pinwheel. Use different colors for each blade or color the opposite blades alike. Try coloring in stripes. Remember to color the back part of each blade.

Instead of a plastic straw you can make a pinwheel stick from a wooden dowel rod or a Tinkertoy stick. Ask an adult to press the pin into a wooden stick.

Button Spinners

No one knows who made the first button spinner. Your great great grandmother may have made one and her grandmother probably taught her how.

To make a button spinner, you need a large button and about 3 feet of string. The bigger the button and the thinner the string the better. Don't try to construct a spinner unless the button is at least 1 inch across. Nylon sewing thread works with 1-inch buttons. Don't use cotton thread. It breaks too easily.

Thread the thin string through the holes in the button, as shown in Illus. 128. Tie the ends so you have the button on a loop of string. If the button has four holes, run the string or thread through two holes farthest apart.

Place your thumbs or middle fingers in each end of the loop. Spin the button around and around between your hands. This puts many twists in the loops. When you have done this about ten or twelve times, pull your hands apart firmly. As the twisted string unwinds the button should spin. The weight of the button will cause it to begin winding the string in the opposite direction. Let your hands come together as the button rewinds the string. The instant it slows down, pull your hands apart again. This reverses the direction the button is spinning.

Illus. 128

If all goes well, your hands begin to move together and apart. The button winds itself up, then unwinds. The faster you spread and close your hands the faster the button spins. The button may even make a little whirring sound.

Once your button is spinning nicely, touch the edge lightly to a countertop or the cover of a book. Remember to keep your hands moving. Depending on the surface the edge of the button touches, you will make different sounds. The button will hop and skip as well.

Color Twirler

A color twirler works a lot like a button spinner, but it's more colorful to watch. Cut out a cardboard disc about 6 or 7 inches across. It must be absolutely round, so use a compass or draw the bottom of a coffee can, a dish, or bowl.

With the point of a compass, poke two small holes in the disc, exactly the same distance from the middle and in line with each other (Illus. 129). Put each hole ½ inch from the middle of the disc. Be careful not to poke your finger. If a compass is not handy, use a ball-point pen to make the holes.

Use colored pencils or crayons to color your spinner. Color half of it blue and the other half red. When this is

Illus. 129

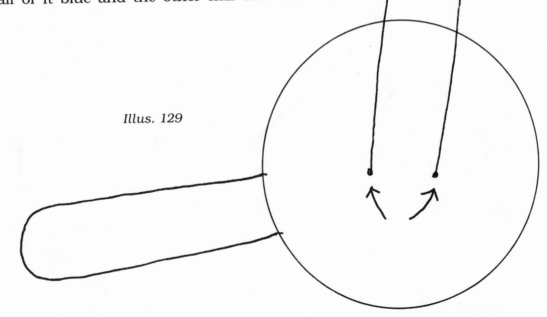

done cut a piece of string about 3 feet long. Thread the ends through the holes in the spinner as you did for the button spinner. Tie the ends together. You now have a loop of string coming out each side of the color spinner.

Work the color spinner just like a button spinner (see page 98).

What happens to the red and blue colors? Look at the spinner as it gains speed. The red and blue blend together and form a different color. What is it?

Make another spinner with two other colors. You may even want to try three colors. Experiment and see what you discover.

Huff-and-Puff Whirligig

This is a simple little spinner that you can make in a jiffy. Cut a 2-inch square out of a file card or other stiff piece of paper. A manila file folder, lightweight poster board, or a piece cut out of a cereal or cracker box works just fine.

Place it in front of you as shown in Illus. 130. Fold point number 2 towards you along the dotted line and crease it so that the fold is at a 90-degree angle to the rest of the square. Fold and crease point 3 away from you in the same

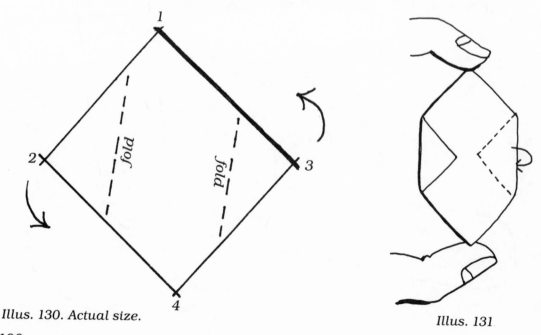

Illus. 130. Actual size.

Illus. 131

way. That's all there is to it. Your huff-and-puff whirligig is ready to use (Illus. 131).

Hold points 1 and 4 against the ball of your thumb and middle finger. Blow gently so the stream of air strikes one of the folded points. Adjust the pressure of your thumb and finger and blow until the whirligig starts to turn. The harder you blow the faster it spins. If you blow too hard, it will fly off into space, still spinning.

To make it turn in the opposite direction, just turn the whirligig upside down.

Try holding it with one end in the palm of your hand and the other end steadied by the finger of your other hand. You can easily think of many other ways to try to hold the whirligig.

When the points get bent and limp just cut out a new one. Try whirligigs of different sizes. Change the shape from a square to a rectangle. Different sizes and shapes perform in a variety of ways. Plastic cut from a liquid soap container makes a good spinner, but sometimes it is hard to make the folds stay in place.

Illus. 132

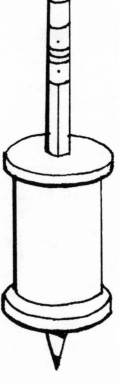

Tops and Spinners

Tops and spinners can provide you with hours of entertainment. A simple top is easy to make and even easier to use.

To make a top, you need a small spool and a pencil about 4 inches long. Slip the pencil through the hole in the spool so that about ¼ or ½ inch of the pointed end sticks out. If the hole in the spool is larger than the pencil, wrap a small piece of paper around the pencil. Then push it through the spool (Illus. 132).

Take the top of the pencil between your thumb and fingers and give it a fast twist. Then let go of the pencil so the top is free. It should spin for several seconds. Some people hold the pencil between the palms of both hands and use a rapid rubbing motion to start the top spinning.

Don't try to spin your top on an extremely slick surface. If the pencil point slides, put a sheet of paper on the surface. Then spin the top on the paper.

Illus. 133

This project is tops!

Oh brother—a comedian you're not!

Make certain the spool is near the point of the pencil. This keeps the center of gravity low and the top's weight just over the pencil point. If the spool is too close to the eraser of the pencil, your top will just roll over and spin on its side.

You may use a pointed dowel instead of a pencil. A pointed dowel and spool from a Tinkertoys set can also be used to make a top.

Plenty of things make dandy spinners. Try spinning a nickel or quarter by standing it on its edge and flicking it with your index finger (Illus. 133). A coin will spin on a slick surface far longer than you expect. Metal washers spin as well as coins, by the way.

A jack from a ball-and-jacks game makes a fantastic spinner (Illus. 133). Hold the pointed end of a jack between your thumb and forefinger and spin the opposite end on a flat surface.

Try to see how many coins or washers or jacks you can keep spinning at one time. Have contests with your friends to see who can keep their spinners going the longest.

Wind Whirler

To make a wind whirler, you need a 4 × 6 file card. A piece of manila folder or even a piece cut from a cereal box will also work fine. Don't use thin paper.

Set your compass so the points are ¼ inch apart. Draw this small circle in the middle of your file card. Now set the compass points 1½ inches apart and draw the second circle around the smaller one. Make sure to use the same middle point for all the circles. Expand the compass points to 1¾ inches and draw a third circle around the second.

Without changing the compass, set the point anywhere on the outer circle. Draw a small arc on that circle. Now set the compass point in that arc and draw another arc on the outside circle. Keep doing this until you work your way around the outside circle.

Using a ruler, draw three straight lines through the middle of the circle to connect these points. Each line connects two of the six points on the circle. Your whirler should look like Illus. 134.

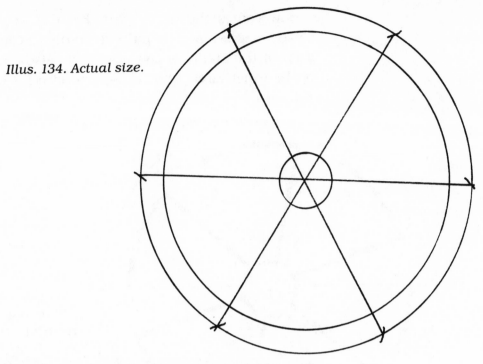

Illus. 134. Actual size.

From each line you just drew, measure exactly ½ inch along the arc of the second circle and make a mark. Place the edge of your ruler along one of these points and the middle of the circles. Draw a line connecting the inner and second circles. Do this for all six sections of the spinner.

Your wind whirler should now look like Illus. 135.

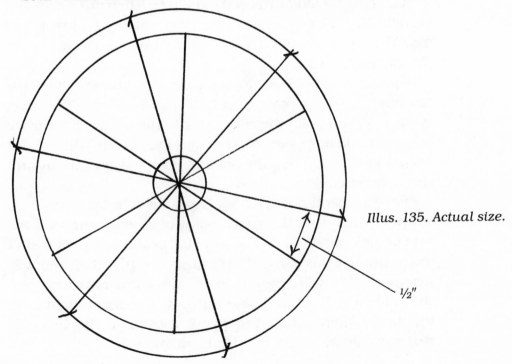

Illus. 135. Actual size.

½"

Now comes the tricky part. For this you need patience, steady nerves, and a pair of pointed scissors. Cut along each of the six lines you just drew. Also cut along the arcs of the inner circle and the second circle, as shown in Illus. 136.

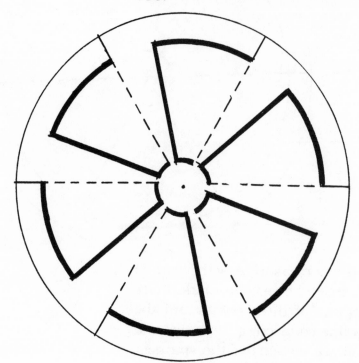

Illus. 136. Put your circle over this pattern and trace the heavy lines. Cut them and fold the flaps downwards along the dotted lines.

Start cutting along the second circle. Then cut down the straight line. Finally, make the tiny cut along the inside circle. When these cuts are finished, fold the flap down along the remaining line.

Repeat this six times to complete the whirler. Don't get too upset if you happen to get a little rip or tear. This may happen as you poke the scissors into the circle. Use a piece of tape to make repairs on the back side of the whirler and keep on cutting. The tape will not ruin it. Now cut around the outside circle.

After you bend down all six flaps, the whirler is ready to whirl. Gently push the sharp point of a pencil through the middle hole made by the steel point of the compass. Don't make the hole very big. (Don't push the pencil all the way through. That will really ruin it!) After you have enlarged the middle hole a little, place the wind whirler lightly on the pencil point. Just the tip of the point should come through, allowing the whirler to turn easily.

Blow gently on the whirler and watch it turn (Illus. 137). Try blowing down from above. Blow from the side. Blow at an angle. You may want to make a larger, heavier wind whirler to use outdoors. If you wish to color the spinner and its flaps, do this before you start cutting. It is just easier to do that way.

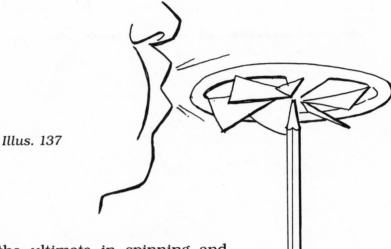

Illus. 137

Mobile

Mobiles are just about the ultimate in spinning and twirling projects. They may be simple or very complex. Mobiles do not have to be made in any exact form. You can use a variety of shapes and all the imagination in the world.

There are two basic rules which must be followed to make your mobile. Begin to build it from the bottom upwards. Make sure that each piece or arm balances before going on to the next one. It's as simple as that.

For this mobile, you will need four pieces of fairly stiff wire, five pieces of stiff cardboard, and a pair of pliers. Pliers with narrow ends are best but almost any type will work.

Begin by drawing the five shapes onto cardboard or stiff file folders. Don't worry about making your mobile shapes exactly like those shown in Illus. 138. You can make them in any shape. Use your own imagination and have fun. In general, large mobile pieces work better than very small ones. They are easier to work with and their larger surfaces catch the breeze better.

If you want to color your mobile pieces, do it before you cut them out. Remember to color both sides. Cut the pieces out with a scissors. Put the pieces aside for now.

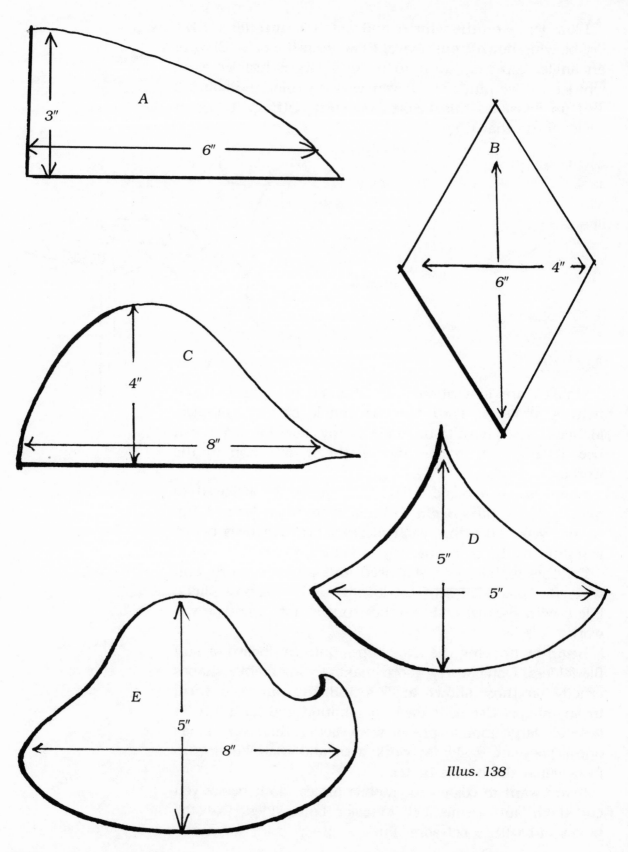

A

3"

6"

B

4"

6"

C

4"

8"

D

5"

5"

E

5"

8"

Illus. 138

You will need four pieces of wire for this mobile. Don't try to use coat hangers. That wire is usually too stiff to work with easily. The first piece should be 12 inches long. Make the second wire 19 inches. The third is 24 inches and the last piece is 25 inches.

Use your fingers and thumbs to shape each wire into a gentle curve. It is possible to make mobiles using straight wires, but the curves make the job easier and look better as well. Use the pliers to form a loop at the end of each wire. Your four wires should look like the ones in Illus. 139.

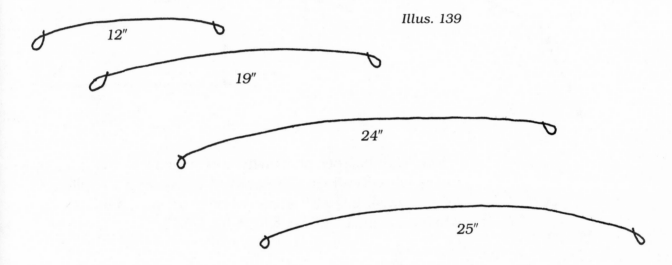

Illus. 139

The next step is to find the balance point for each of the five cardboard pieces. One way to do this is to prop a ruler on one edge and place each piece of cardboard on the top edge. Move the piece until it balances on the edge of the ruler. Mark that spot with a little pencil mark. Then punch a little hole about ⅛ inch from the top of this balance point. (The approximate balance points are shown in the five mobile drawings as dots near the top.) The exact point of balance depends upon the shape and dimensions of each piece you make. Find all five balance points and punch the holes.

Make a small wire loop for each of the five mobile pieces. This loop should not be more than ½ inch across and may be made smaller. Paper clips make good loops, which you can bend with a pliers. Put a loop through the balance hole of each mobile piece (Illus. 140).

small wire loop

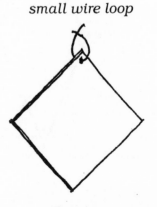

Illus. 140

107

Hook pieces A and B to the ends of the 12-inch wire. Close the loops in the ends of the wire so the pieces will not fall off when the mobile turns. Now use the edge of a ruler to find where the wire balances. Rest the wire on the ruler's edge and move it back and forth until it balances (Illus. 141).

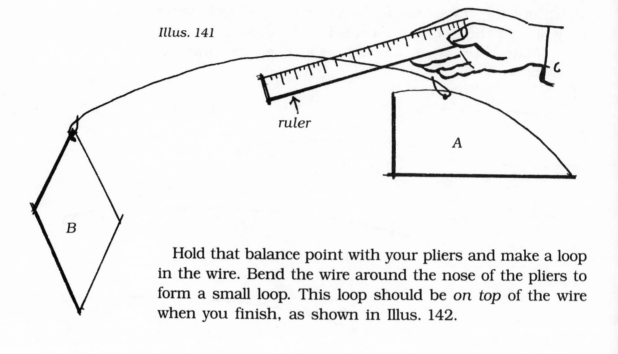

Illus. 141

ruler

Hold that balance point with your pliers and make a loop in the wire. Bend the wire around the nose of the pliers to form a small loop. This loop should be *on top* of the wire when you finish, as shown in Illus. 142.

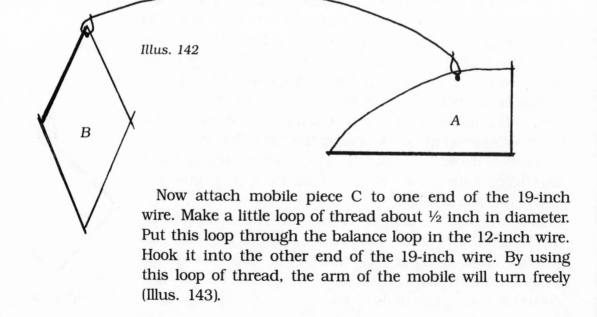

Illus. 142

Now attach mobile piece C to one end of the 19-inch wire. Make a little loop of thread about ½ inch in diameter. Put this loop through the balance loop in the 12-inch wire. Hook it into the other end of the 19-inch wire. By using this loop of thread, the arm of the mobile will turn freely (Illus. 143).

Use the edge of a ruler to find the balance point for the 19-inch wire. Make a loop there with the pliers just as you did for the first wire (Illus. 141).

Illus. 143

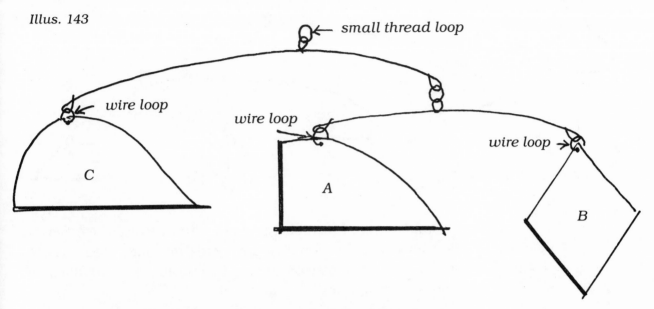

Next hook mobile piece D to one end of the 24-inch wire. Make another ½-inch thread loop and attach it to the other end of the wire. Hook the thread loop in the balance loop of the 19-inch wire. Again, use the ruler's edge to locate the balance point for the 24-inch wire. Make the balance loop just as you did before.

The next step is to attach mobile piece E to one end of the 25-inch wire. Using another thread loop, fasten the other end of the wire to the balance loop of the 24-inch wire. Your mobile is all but ready to hang.

Finally, use the edge of the ruler to locate the balance point in the 25-inch wire and make the loop. Tie one end of strong thread or string into that loop and attach the other to a hook in the ceiling.

Stand back and admire your mobile as it slowly spins and turns. It should look something like Illus. 144.

Make certain each arm of your mobile balances. If one arm runs into a mobile piece, just make the thread loop longer between the two arms. Use various shapes and sizes for mobile pieces. Experiment with longer and shorter arms.

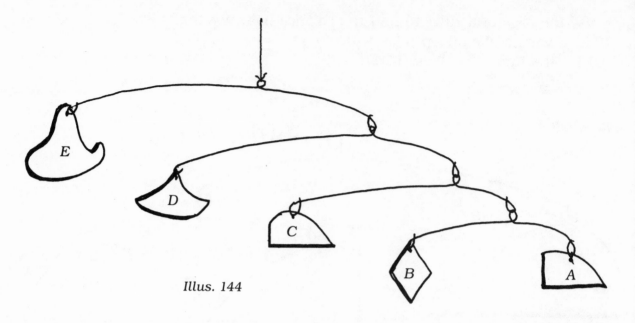

Illus. 144

Build a mobile which uses more than five pieces. Seven is a good number for your next creation (Illus. 145). There is no correct shape or form. Just keep them in balance and anything goes!

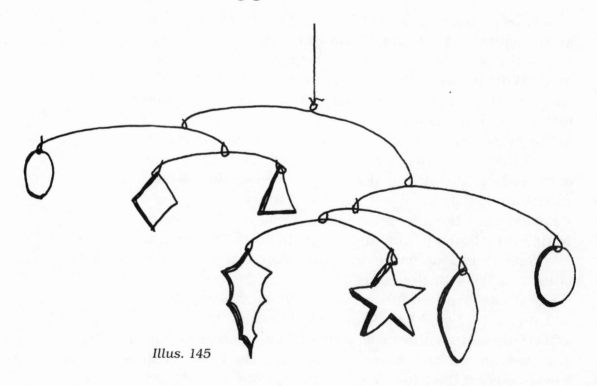

Illus. 145

Index

L

Liquid soap, 87
Looper, 22–25

M

Magic finger trap, 91–92
Manila folders, toys made with, 13, 67, 100, 102
Masking tape, 43, 53, 92, 94, 104
Matchboxes, toys made with, 34
Mobiles, 105–110
    balancing, 107–109
    patterns for, 106
    wire for, 107, 108
Musical bottles, 60

N

Newspaper, 40, 84–85
Noisemakers, 29–31, 37–63
Nylon cord, 56

P

Palm popper, 44–46
Paper bag, exploding, 46
Paper clips, 13, 15, 18, 49, 75, 76–77, 107
Paper puffer, 83
Parachutes, 75–76
Party hat, 84–85
Pencils, 14, 53, 68, 76, 101, 104
Pinwheel, 97–98
Planes, paper, 15–25
    See also gliders
Plastic straws, 11–12, 33–34, 75, 98
    bursting, 47–48
Playing cards, 58–59
Pliers, 105, 107, 109
Popper, paper, 40–44
    See also big-bang paper popper, palm popper

R

Rattles, 48–50
Ring catcher, 72
Rocket, straw-cover, 33–34
Rubber bands, 49
Ruler, 68, 102, 107

S

Scissors, 11, 15, 68, 97, 104, 105
Screamer, 29
Singing glass, 31
Snapper, paper, 37–39
Soap-bottle surprise, 92–93
Soap bubbles, 86–87
Spinners, 101–102
Spools, 86–87, 101
Straws, 11–12, 33–34, 75
    bursting, 47–48

T

Thread, 62, 75, 98, 99–100, 108
Thumbtacks, 14
Tops, 101–102
Tightrope walker, 74
Tinkertoy sticks, 14, 60, 98
Tin-pan band, 61
Tissue paper, 54, 83
Turkey caller, 53–54
Twirlicopter, 13–14

W

Washers, metal, 49, 75
Waxed paper, 54
Whirligig, huff-and-puff, 100
Whirly-twirly, 11–12
Whistle, cellophane, 29–30
Whistle, plastic, 83
Wind chimes, 62–63
Wind whirler, 102–105
Wind woofer, 55–56
Wire, 62, 105